Tableau
Business Intelligence Clinic
Create and Learn

Roger F. Silva

www.createandlearn.net

Roger F. Silva

createandlearn.net

contact.createandlearn@gmail.com

Tableau version: April 2022

ISBN: 9781082135170

Contents

For more **Create and Learn** books and articles visit:
www.createandlearn.net

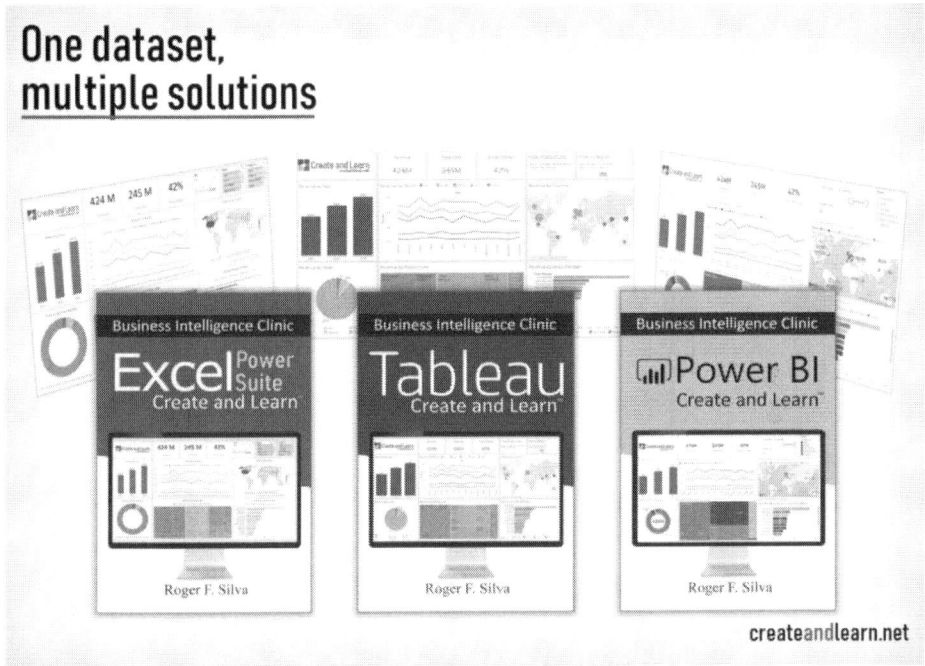

One dataset, multiple solutions

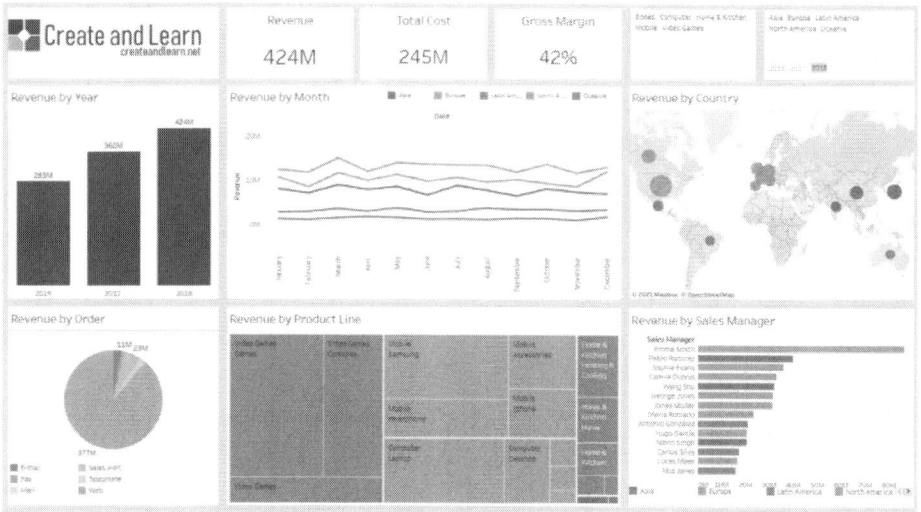

Dashboard to be created: Desktop version

Dashboard to be created: Mobile version

Introduction

Dear Reader,

In this Business Intelligence Clinic series, you will explore various BI solutions.

Each book is about a different BI tool, and you will follow step-by-step instructions to create a professional sales dashboard with the same friendly dataset. This BI Clinic series will help you compare different Business Intelligence tools, learn the basics, and select the best for your project, company, customers, or personal needs.

In this Create and Learn book: Tableau – Business Intelligence Clinic, you will go through important topics of Tableau Desktop. You will learn how to install Tableau Desktop, get data from Excel, model your Data, work with visuals and reports, create a sales dashboard, and share your work with others.

We will not go into deep theories as to the purpose of this book, and all Create and Learn material is to make the most of your time and learn by doing.

You will follow step-by-step instructions to create a professional sales dashboard and eight warm-up dashboards to help you rapidly increase your knowledge.

I hope this book will help you start your journey in the Business Intelligence world and give you the right tools to start building professional reports and dashboards using Tableau.

You can find more here https://www.createandlearn.net/tableau

Thank you for creating and learning.

Roger F. Silva

contact.createandlearn@gmail.com
createandlearn.net
www.linkedin.com/in/roger-f-silva

Chapter 1

Get Started

1. The Business Intelligence Clinic Dataset

The Business Intelligence Clinic dataset is a friendly, easy-to-read set of four tables containing the high-level sales information from a fictitious company, and they will be used in every BI Clinic book.

These are the tables you will find:

Sales: Contains the main sales data in a three-year range. Each row of data represents a single sales transaction.

Region: Contains countries and regions where the company operates.

SalesManager: Contains the sales manager's names by country.

Dates: Contains the dates and group of dates.

2. Business Intelligence and Tableau

The main goal of Business Intelligence is to help people and companies make better decisions, and according to Wikipedia, business intelligence is a set of methodologies, processes, architectures, and technologies that transform raw data into meaningful and useful information used to enable more effective strategic, tactical, and operational insights and decision-making.

Tableau is a Business Intelligence software that allows users to get data from multiple sources, transform the data, and create reports, dashboards, and many types of visualizations.

The user can then share those reports with colleagues and customers across multiple platforms, such as Tableau Online, Tableau Public, PDF, PowerPoint, websites, and more.

Until recently, Business Intelligence solutions were aimed at Enterprise-level BI, with complex and costly products, and most of it was done by IT professionals.

Nowadays, you can find a range of self-service BI solutions, and Tableau is one of them. These solutions allow salespeople, analysts, managers, and a variety of professionals to get data, model the data, create visualizations, and share them.

3. Tableau products

Tableau is a suite of business analytics tools that deliver insights throughout your organization. It allows you to connect to hundreds of data sources, simplify data preparation, and drive ad hoc analysis. You can produce beautiful reports, then publish them for your organization to consume on the web and across mobile devices.

The main Tableau products are:

Tableau Desktop: This is the main tool used in this book. It has a free trial option, it is installed in the computer, and allows users to connect the data, prepare and model the data, create reports, and run advanced analytics.

Tableau Prep: It is used for data preparation or data cleaning to get the data ready for analysis. Tableau Prep is comprised of two products; Tableau Prep Builder for building your data flows and Tableau Prep

Conductor for sharing flows and managing them across the organization.

Tableau Server: This is a larger enterprise-level solution. It shares the visuals created in Tableau Desktop.

Tableau Online: It is a hosted version of Tableau Server.

Tableau Public: This is a free solution, which hosts a public gallery of visuals. After published, everyone can see your visualizations. Don't use this if you have sensitive data.

4. Install Tableau Desktop

To install Tableau on your computer, go to the Tableau website; currently, the address is https://www.tableau.com/.

You will find multiple choice of getting to the download page on the Tableau website, such as **Products**, **Try Now**, and others.

Note: If you have already installed the trial version of Tableau Desktop in your computer and it has expired, you will have to use the full version or the **Tableau Public** available at https://public.tableau.com ; and some functions presented in this book (chapter 8 and 10) are not available in the Public version.

1. To install Tableau Desktop, go to **Products** and select **Tableau Desktop** as the image below.

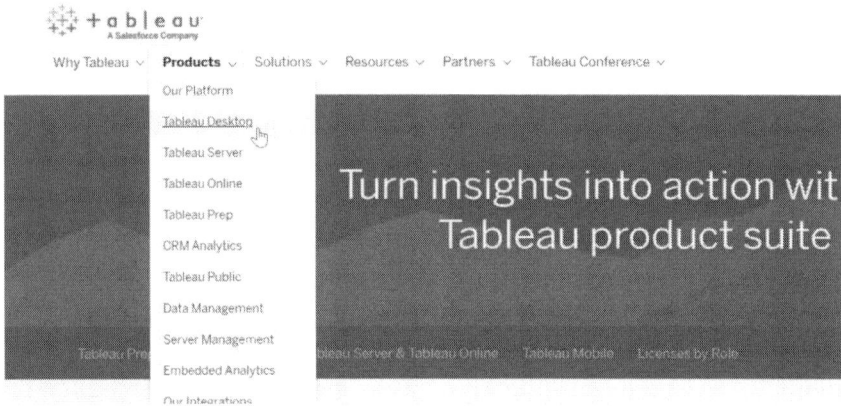

2. Then, Click on **TRY IT FOR FREE**.

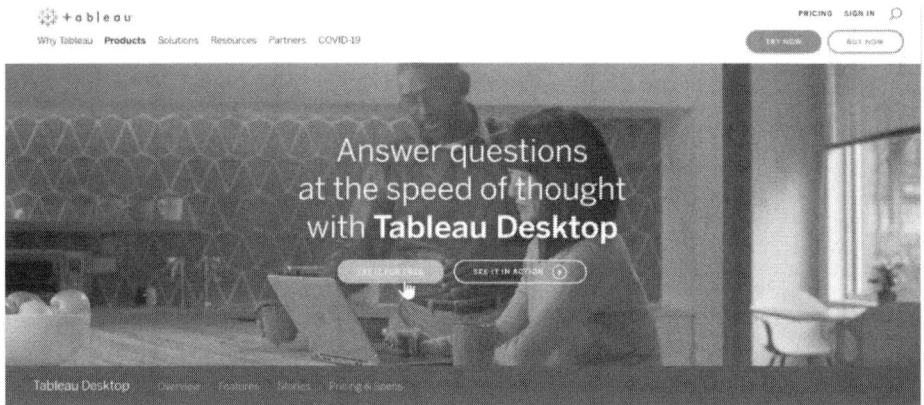

3. Fill the download form and click on **Download Free Trial**. You will have 14 days to use the trial. Then you can choose to buy the license or use the free version **Tableau Public** (the data and reports will be available to the general public). Your computer will download the installation file.

Phone (e.g. (201) 555-0123)

By registering, you confirm that you agree to the processing of your personal data by Salesforce as described in the Privacy Statement.

DOWNLOAD FREE TRIAL

WE RESPECT YOUR PRIVACY | HAVING TROUBLE?

STUDENT OR TEACHER? GET A FREE 1-YEAR LICENSE. LEARN MORE

4. Open the file to start installing Tableau. Check the license terms if you agree and click on **Install**.

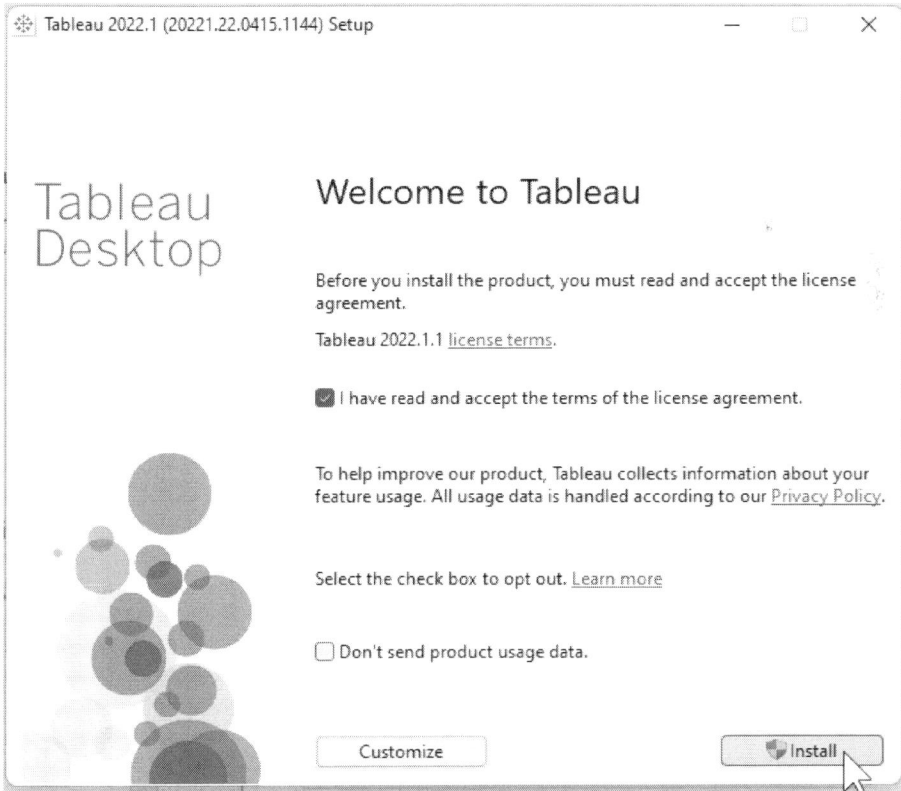

Tableau 2022.1 (20221.22.0415.1144) Setup — □ ×

Tableau
Desktop

Welcome to Tableau

Before you install the product, you must read and accept the license agreement.

Tableau 2022.1.1 license terms.

☑ I have read and accept the terms of the license agreement.

To help improve our product, Tableau collects information about your feature usage. All usage data is handled according to our Privacy Policy.

Select the check box to opt out. Learn more

☐ Don't send product usage data.

Customize   💎 Install

5. Tableau will request you to fill a Registration to use the free trial during the installation process. Fill the form and click on **Start trial now**.

Tableau Registration   ✕

Almost there

Have a product key? Activate Tableau

First name   Last name

Business email   Organization

Department
--   ▼

Job Role
--   ▼

Country/Region
United States   ▼

State
--   ▼

ZIP code

Phone (e.g. (201) 555-5555)

Start trial now

We respect your privacy | Having trouble?

6. Tableau should start automatically. If not, double click the icon on your desktop

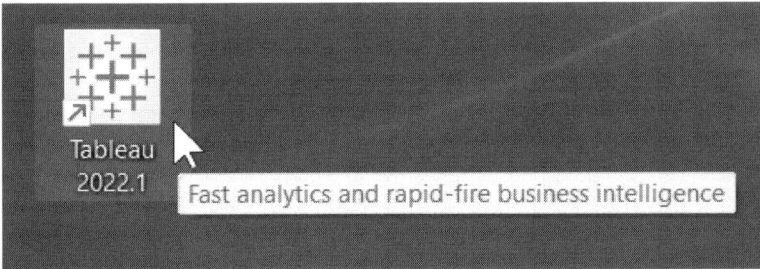

7. The welcome screen will appear similar to the image below.

Chapter 2

Connect to the Sales Data

Before you begin your analysis, you must connect to your data and then set up the data source. With Tableau, you can connect to different data sources and types. You can use from basic sources of data such as CSV files and spreadsheets, till SQL server, services from Amazon, Tableau server, and much more.

1. Visit the address <u>createandlearn.net/bifiles</u> download the Excel file **SalesData.xlsx** and the Create and Learn **Image**. The xlsx file contains the dataset that you will use to create the visuals and the dashboard.

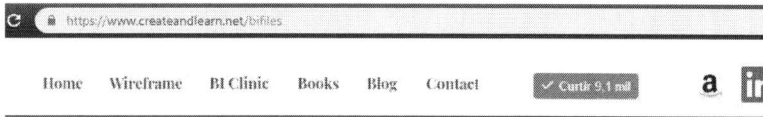

Book material:

Right–click the image and click on **Save image as**

2. Go to **Connect**, **To a File** and click on **Microsoft Excel**.

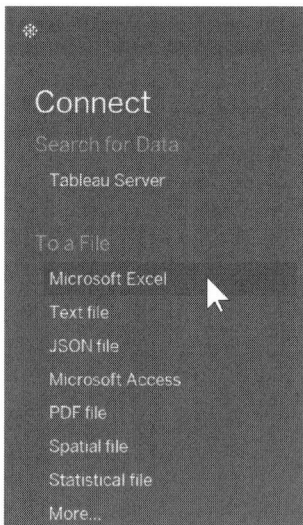

3. Select the file you have downloaded **SalesData.xlsx,** and click on
Open.

File name:	SalesData	⌄	Excel Workbooks (*.xls *.xlsx *.⤳ ⌄
		Open	Cancel

4. Tableau will open the data source page and will show on the left the
connection it has created called **SalesData**, and all the four tabs:
Dates, **Region**, **Sales,** and **Sales Manager**

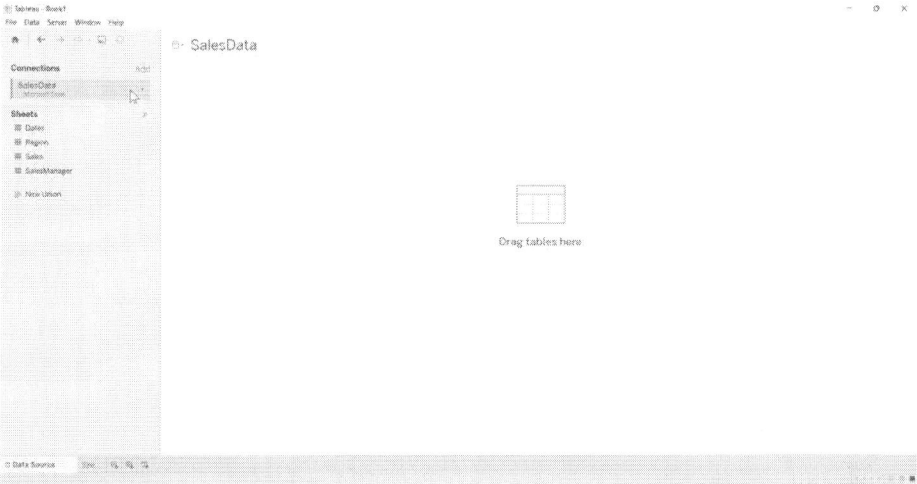

5. Go to **Sheets** session and drag the sheet **Sales** to the **canvas** (Drag tables here) as in the image below.

6. You can see the data from the **Sales** tab, down below in the grid and ready to be used.

Retailer co...	Order meth...	Product line	Product type	Date	Quantity	Price	Revenue	Unit Cost
France	Telephone	Computer	Laptop	1/1/2016	56	1,397.94	78,284.61	772.352
United States	Telephone	Computer	Laptop	1/1/2016	89	1,397.94	124,416.61	724.832
Brazil	Web	Mobile	Iphone	1/1/2016	23	924.64	21,266.70	518.723
Mexico	Sales visit	Mobile	Samsung	1/1/2016	48	750.79	36,037.80	472.245
China	Web	Mobile	Samsung	1/1/2016	77	643.86	49,577.40	388.571
Japan	E-mail	Mobile	Samsung	1/1/2016	43	652.44	28,054.80	388.200
United States	Web	Mobile	Samsung	1/1/2016	125	507.29	63,411.30	306.150
Spain	Web	Mobile	Samsung	1/1/2016	47	506.47	23,804.10	301.350
Italy	Web	Computer	Laptop	1/1/2016	28	382.95	10,722.60	218.090
France	Telephone	Mobile	Samsung	1/1/2016	44	320.13	14,085.90	217.891
Japan	Web	Video Games	Consoles	1/1/2016	88	271.18	23,863.50	156.740
Canada	Web	Video Games	Consoles	1/1/2016	66	225.61	14,758.20	117.842
Japan	Web	Video Games	Consoles	1/1/2016	114	222.56	25,371.90	138.099

7. To create relationships between tables; Drag the tab **Region** to the grid as well. Note, that Tableau will try to create a relationship identified as a line between the tables.

8. Go to the **Edit Relationship** window, and select **Retailer country** on the Sales side. Then go to Region side and select **Country**. This will tell Tableau to connect the tables through their common **Country** key.

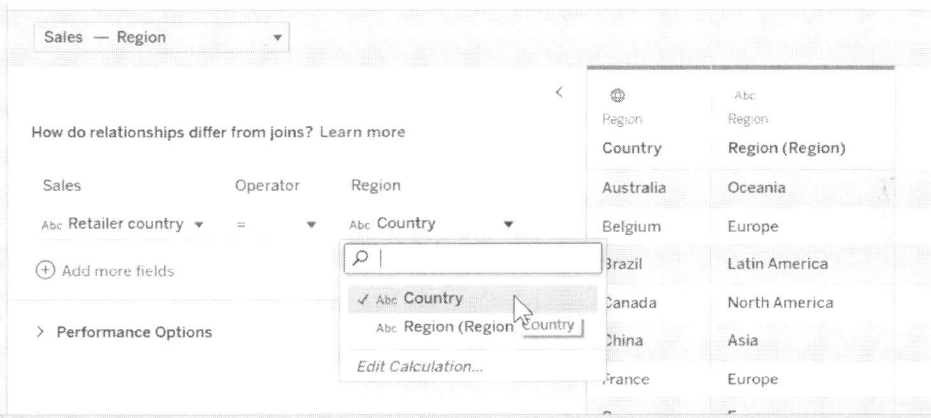

9. Drag the tab **SalesManager** to the grid as in the image below. Go to the **Edit Relationship** window and select country on the Region side. Then go to **Sales Manager** side and select **Country (SalesManager)**.

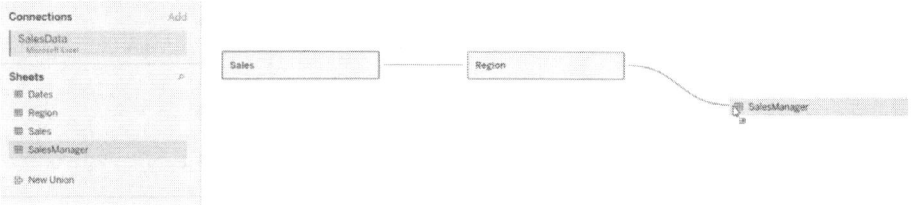

10. Tableau should find the relationship automatically for the SalesManager table.

11. Drag the tab **Dates** to the grid.

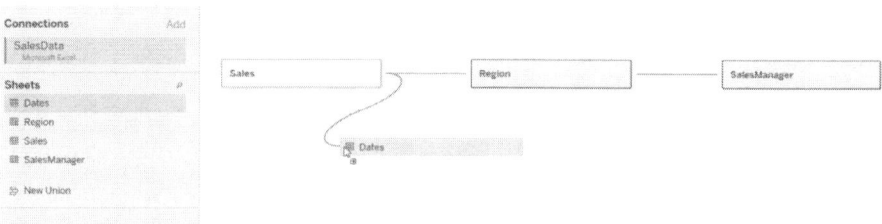

12. Go to **Edit Relationship** window, and on the **Sales** side, select **Date**. Then go to **Dates** side and select **Full Date**.

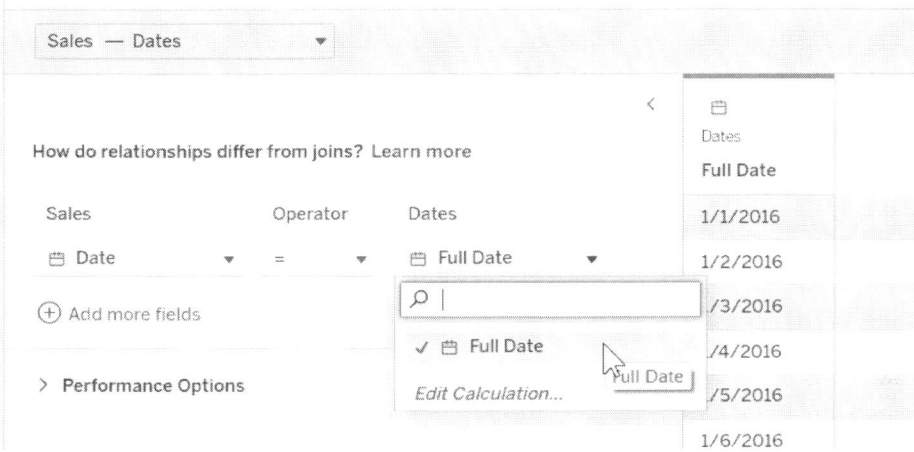

Sales — Dates			

			<	Dates
How do relationships differ from joins? Learn more				Full Date
				1/1/2016
Sales	Operator	Dates		1/2/2016
Date ▼	= ▼	Full Date ▼		/3/2016
⊕ Add more fields		✓ Full Date		/4/2016
		Edit Calculation...	Full Date	/5/2016
> Performance Options				1/6/2016

13. In this model, we want all **dimension tables** (Date, Region, and SalesManager) connected to the **fact table** (Sales). Drag the **SalesManager** table to **Sales** as in the image below.

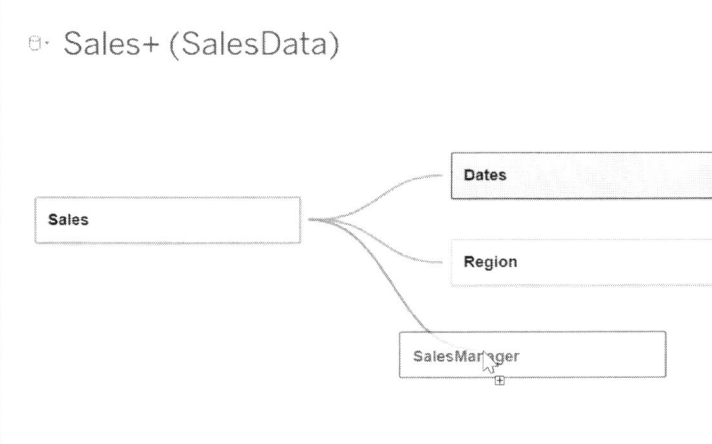

Sales+ (SalesData)

Dates

Sales

Region

SalesManager

14. Go to **Edit Relationship** window, and on the Sales side, select **Retailer Country**. Then go to the SalesManager side and select **Country (SalesManager).**

e· Sales+ (SalesData)

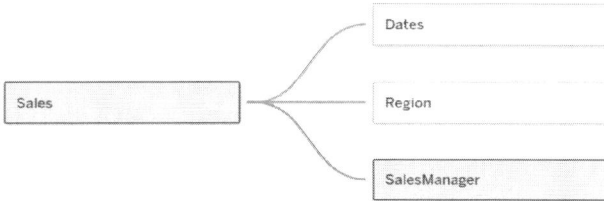

Sales		Dates
		Region
		SalesManager

Sales — SalesMan...	▼					
				<	⊕ SalesManager	Abc SalesManager
How do relationships differ from joins? Learn more					Country (SalesManager)	Sales Manager
					Australia	Mia Jones
Sales	Operator	SalesManager			Belgium	Lucas Maes
Abc Retailer country ▼	= ▼	Abc Country (SalesM ▼			Brazil	Carlos Silva
		⌕			Canada	Sophia Evans
⊕ Add more fields		✓ Abc Country (SalesManager)				Wang Shu
		Abc Sales Manager		Country (SalesManager)		
> Performance Options		Edit Calculation...			France	Camila Dubois

15. The relationships should look like the image below.

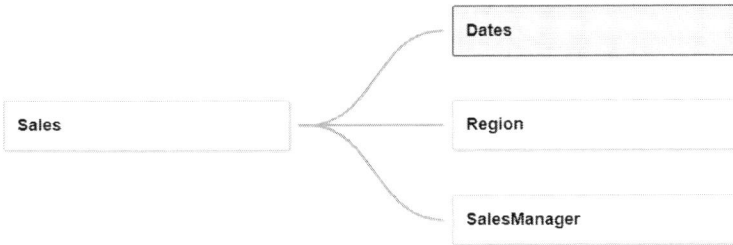

Sales+ (SalesData)

16. Go to **File** and click on **Save As**.

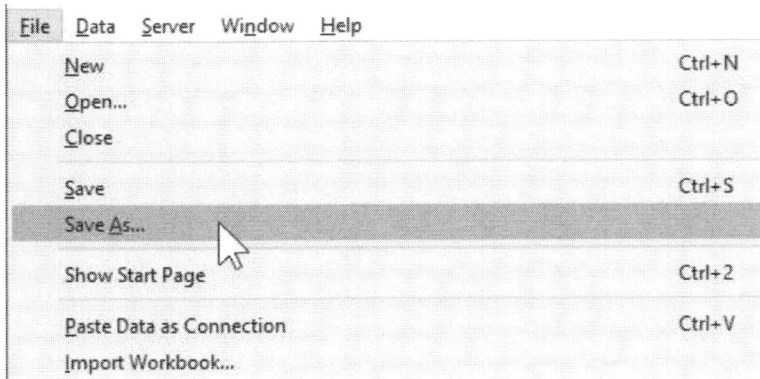

17. Rename the file to **Tableau BI Clinic – Create and Learn** and click on **Save**.

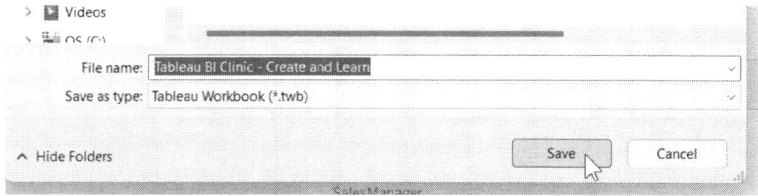

> ■ Videos	
> ■ OS (C:)	

File name:	Tableau BI Clinic - Create and Learn
Save as type:	Tableau Workbook (*.twb)

∧ Hide Folders   **Save**   Cancel

Chapter 3

Creating Calculated Fields

1. Go to the bottom and click on **Sheet 1**.

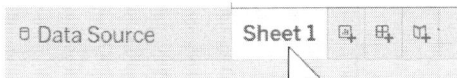

2. Go to **Window** and make sure to have the **Show Toolbar**, **Show Status Bar,** and **Show Side Bar** activated.

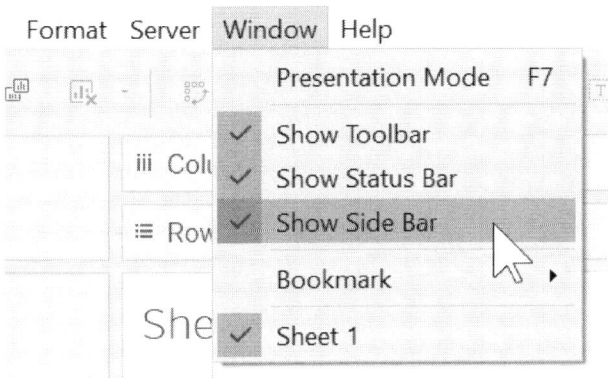

4. Below you will find an official description from the Tableau team of the workspace area.

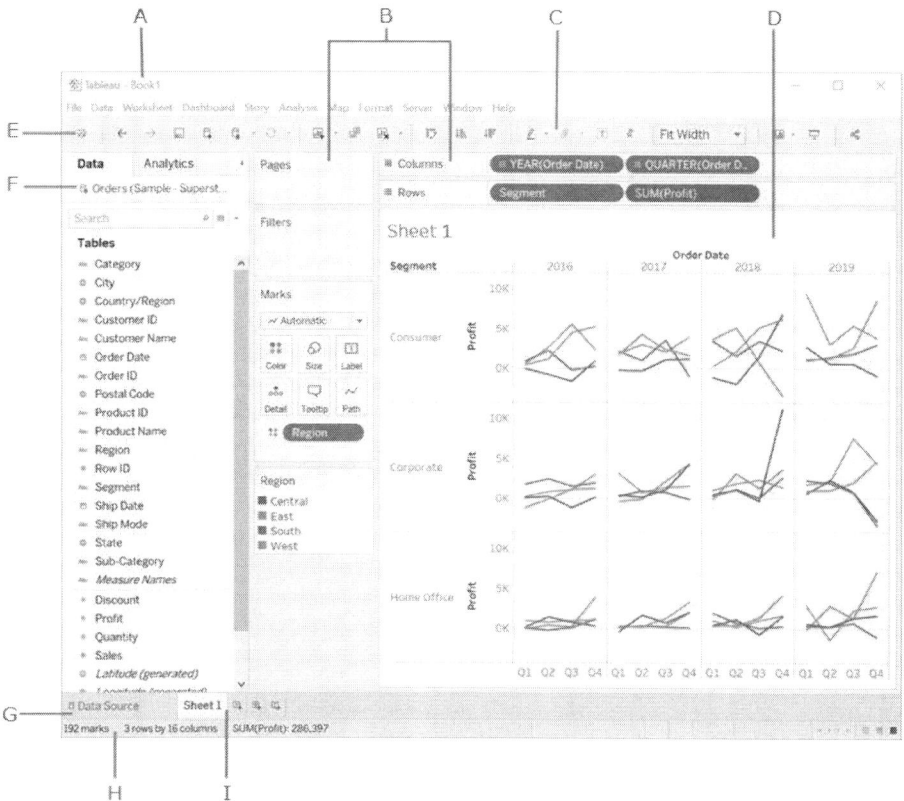

A. Workbook name. A workbook contains sheets. A sheet can be a worksheet, a dashboard, or a story. For more information, see Workbooks and Sheets.

B. Cards and shelves - Drag fields to the cards and shelves in the workspace to add data to your view.

C. Toolbar - Use the toolbar to access commands and analysis and navigation tools.

D. View - This is the canvas in the workspace where you create a visualization (also referred to as a "viz").

E. Click this icon to go to the Start page, where you can connect to data. For more information, see Start Page.

F. Side Bar - In a worksheet, the side bar area contains the Data pane and the Analytics pane.

G. Click this tab to go to the Data Source page and view your data. For more information, see Data Source Page.

H. Status bar - Displays information about the current view.

I. Sheet tabs - Tabs represent each sheet in your workbook. This can include worksheets, dashboards, and stories. For more information, see Workbooks and Sheets.

5. The columns from the imported data are shown as fields on the Data Pane's left side in the worksheet.

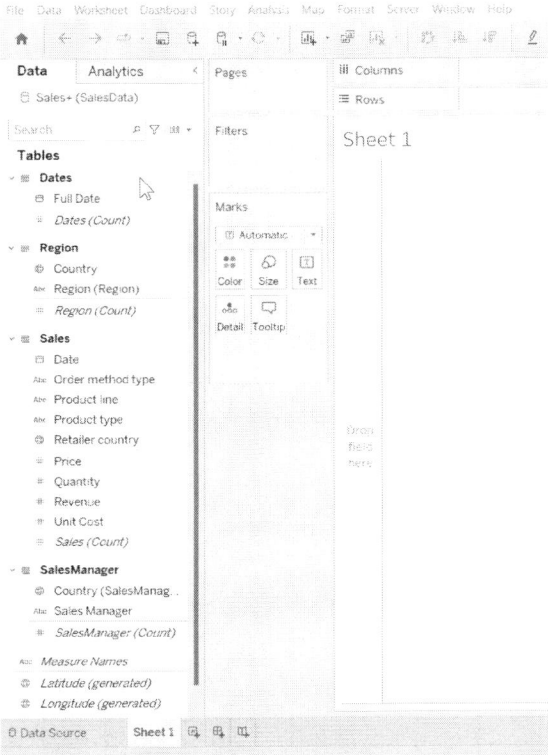

6. Go to Analysis and click on Create Calculated Field.

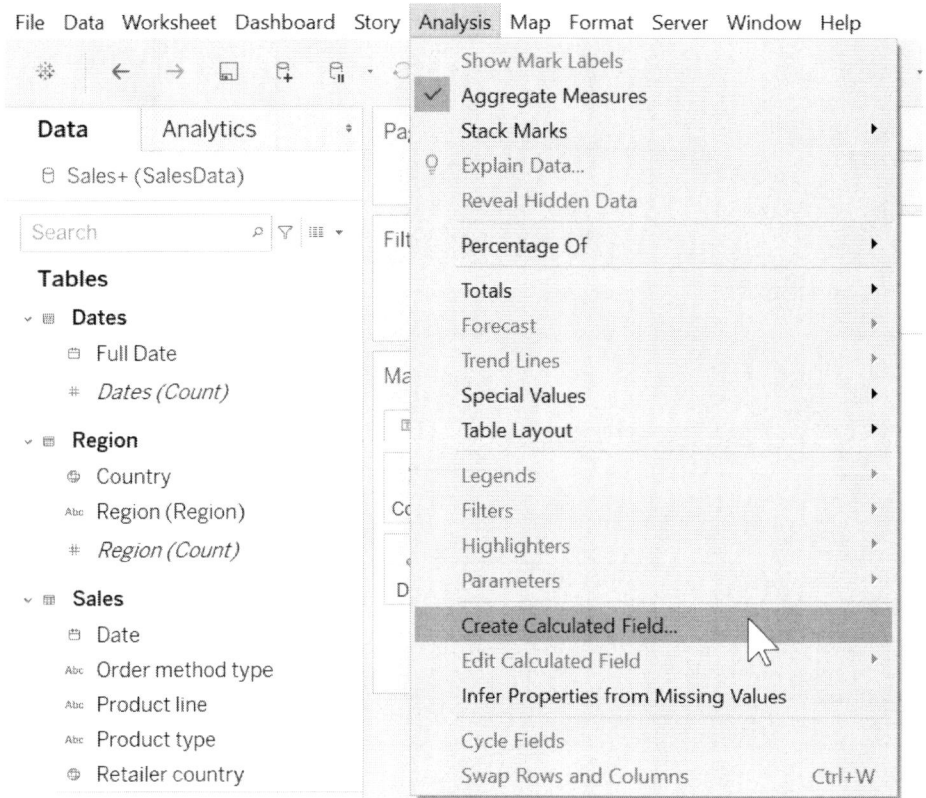

7. In the calculation editor that opens, insert the field name **Total Cost**. Click on the white area and include the formula **[Unit Cost] * [Quantity].** Then, click **OK.**

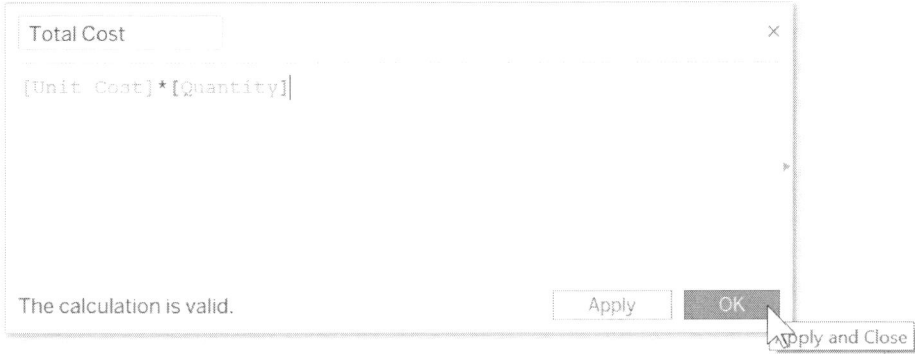

Total Cost	×

[Unit Cost]*[Quantity]|

| The calculation is valid. | Apply | OK |

Apply and Close

See the explanation:

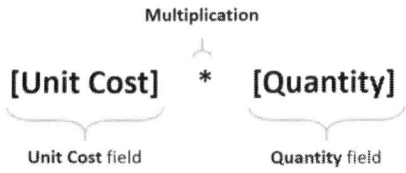

Multiplication

[Unit Cost]   *   **[Quantity]**

Unit Cost field   **Quantity** field

8. The new calculated field will be added to the Data pane.

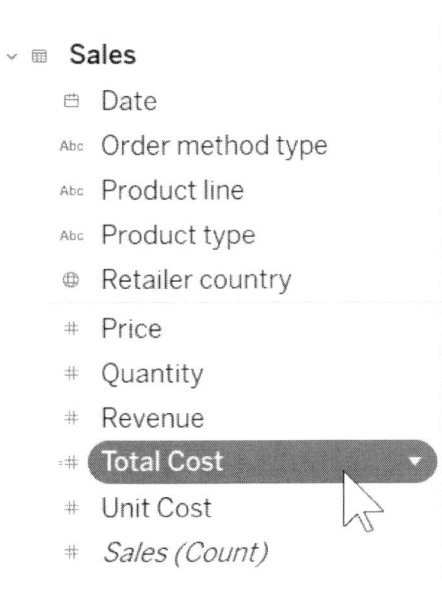

∨ ▦ **Sales**

   🖬 Date

   Abc Order method type

   Abc Product line

   Abc Product type

   ⊕ Retailer country

   # Price

   # Quantity

   # Revenue

   # Total Cost ▾

   # Unit Cost

   # *Sales (Count)*

10. Go to Analysis and click on Create Calculated Field.

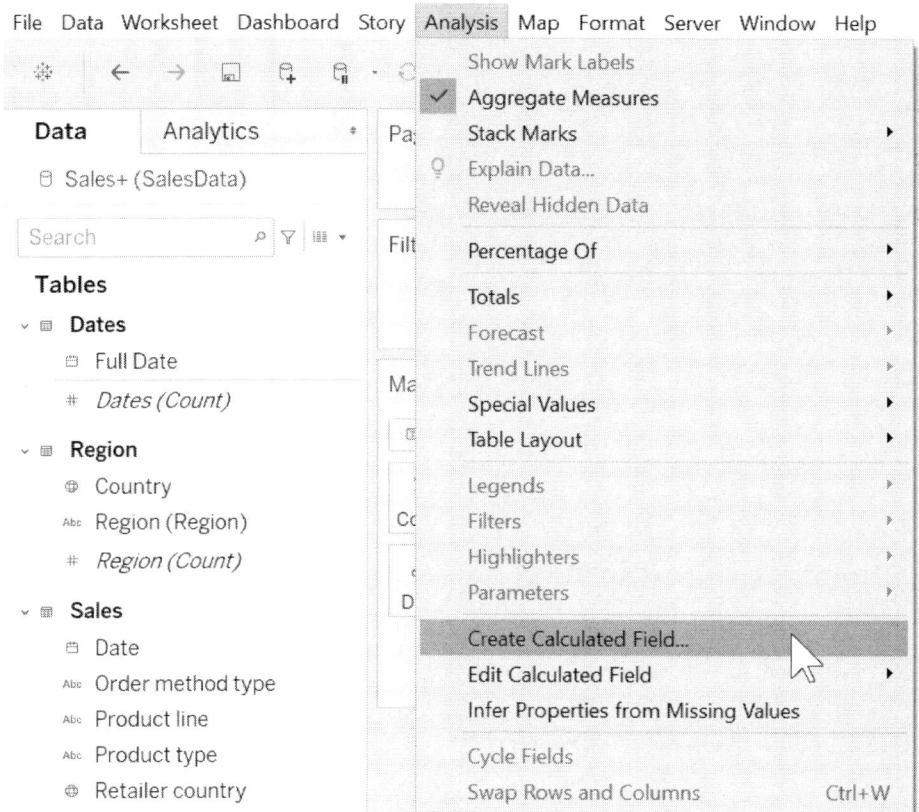

File   Data   Worksheet   Dashboard   Story   **Analysis**   Map   Format   Server   Window   Help

Analysis menu
Show Mark Labels
✓ Aggregate Measures
Stack Marks ▸
🔍 Explain Data...
Reveal Hidden Data
Percentage Of ▸
Totals ▸
Forecast ▸
Trend Lines ▸
Special Values ▸
Table Layout ▸
Legends ▸
Filters ▸
Highlighters ▸
Parameters ▸
Create Calculated Field...
Edit Calculated Field ▸
Infer Properties from Missing Values
Cycle Fields
Swap Rows and Columns   Ctrl+W

Data   Analytics

⊟ Sales+ (SalesData)

Search

Tables

∨ ▦ **Dates**
  ▤ Full Date
  # *Dates (Count)*

∨ ▦ **Region**
  ⊕ Country
  Abc Region (Region)
  # *Region (Count)*

∨ ▦ **Sales**
  ▤ Date
  Abc Order method type
  Abc Product line
  Abc Product type
  ⊕ Retailer country

11. In the calculation editor that opens, insert the field name **Gross Margin**. Click on the white area and include the formula **(sum([Revenue])-sum([Total Cost]))/sum([Revenue])** . Then click **OK.**

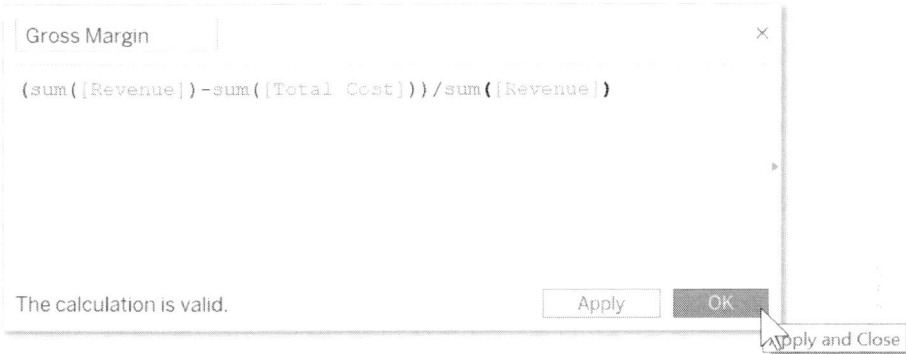

Gross Margin	×

(sum([Revenue])-sum([Total Cost]))/sum([Revenue])

The calculation is valid.   Apply   OK

Apply and Close

See the explanation:

Subtraction   Division

(sum([Revenue]) - sum([Total Cost])) / sum([Revenue])

Sum of the	Sum of the	Sum of the
Revenue Column	**Total Cost** formula	**Revenue** column

The two new calculated fields were added to the Data pane, and they are available to be used.

∨ ▦ **Sales**

　　🗓 Date

　　ᴬᵇᶜ Order method type

　　ᴬᵇᶜ Product line

　　ᴬᵇᶜ Product type

　　⊕ Retailer country

　　# Price

　　# Quantity

　　# Revenue

　　⁼# Total Cost

　　# Unit Cost

　　# *Sales (Count)*

∨ ▦ **SalesManager**

　　⊕ Country (SalesManager)

　　ᴬᵇᶜ Sales Manager

　　# *SalesManager (Count)*

　ᴬᵇᶜ *Measure Names*

　⁼# **Gross Margin**

　⊕ *Latitude (generated)*

　⊕ *Longitude (generated)*

　# *Measure Values*

Chapter 4
Creating Visuals

5. Revenue

1. Go to **Data pane** and click on the **Revenue.**

Tables

- # *Region (Count)*
- ⊞ **Sales**
  - 🗓 Date
  - Abc Order method type
  - Abc Product line
  - Abc Product type
  - 🌐 Retailer country
  - # Price
  - # Quantity
  - # Revenue
  - # Total Cost
  - # Unit Cost
  - # *Sales (Count)*
- ⊞ **SalesManager**
  - 🌐 Country (SalesManager)
  - Abc Sales Manager
  - # *SalesManager (Count)*
- Abc *Measure Names*
- # Gross Margin

2. Drag the **Revenue** pill from the data pane and drop it on **Marks** as in the image below.

3. On the left side of the Revenue pill, you can change the way the data will be displayed.

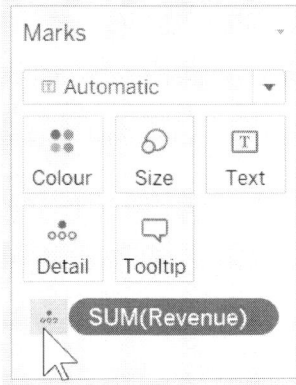

4. Click on the left icon and select **Text** as the image below.

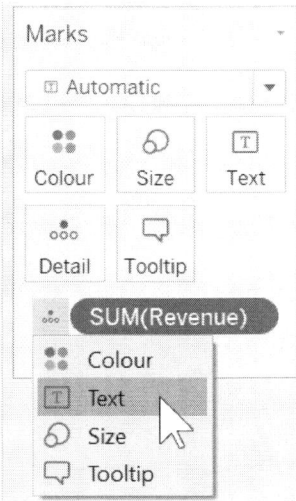

5. The result will be displayed on the **Canvas.**

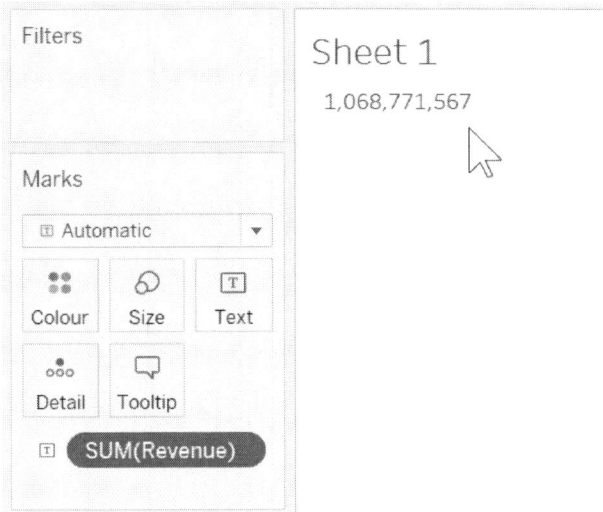

Filters

Marks

| Automatic ▼ |

| Colour | Size | Text |
| Detail | Tooltip |

| SUM(Revenue) |

Sheet 1

1,068,771,567

6. Go to the **Marks** card and click on the **down arrow** inside the **Revenue** pill. Then click on **Format**.

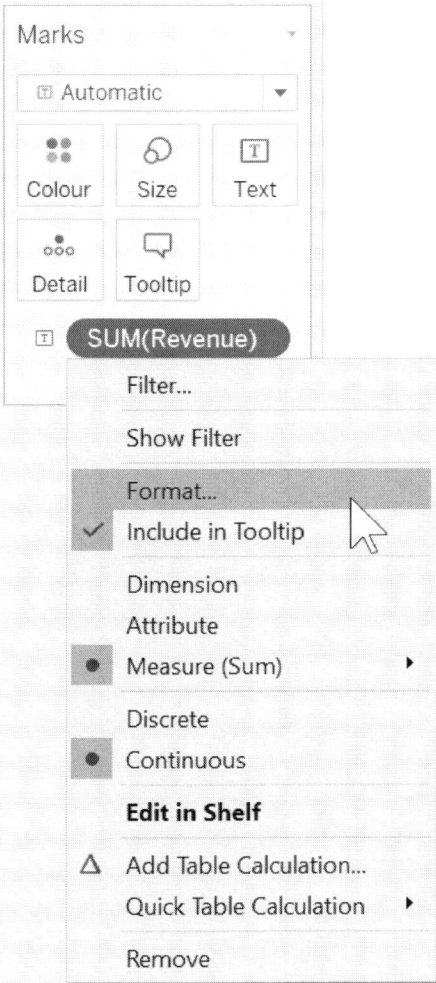

7. Go to the sidebar on the left and click on **Pane** tab.

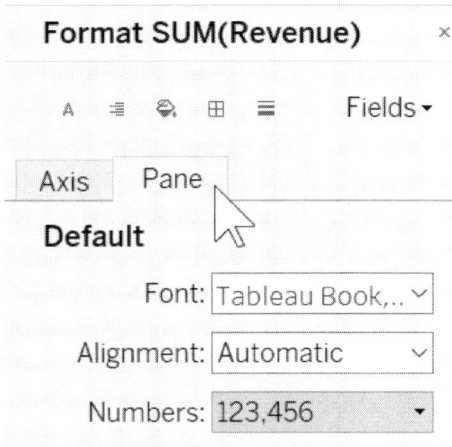

8. Go to **Default**, **Numbers**, and click on **Number Custom**.

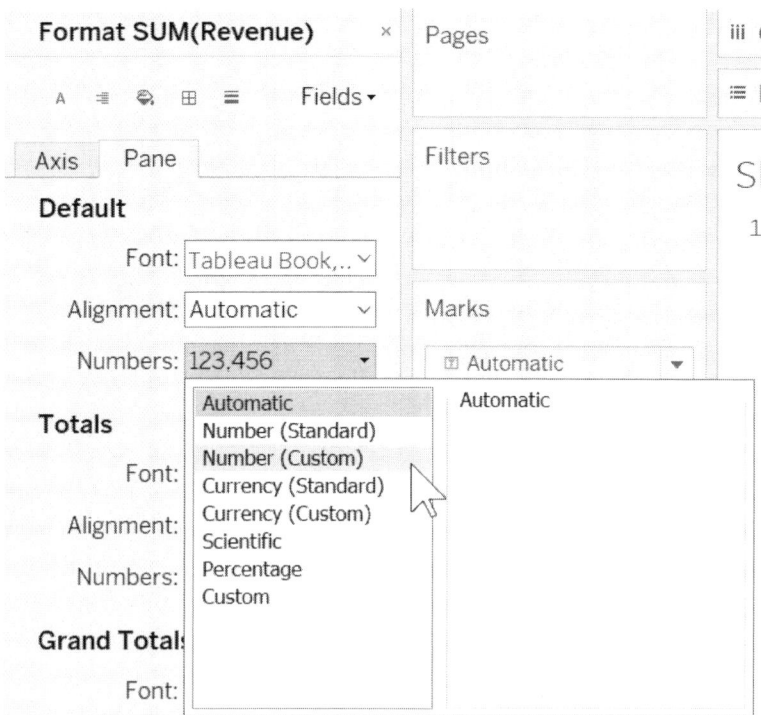

9. Set the decimal places to **Zero** and change the **Display Units** to **Millions (M)**.

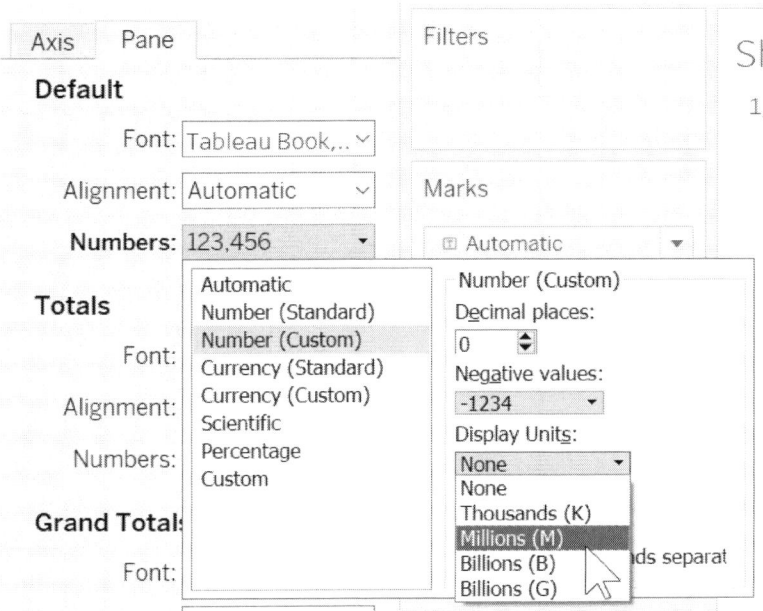

10. Go to **Default**, **Font**, and change the **Font Size** to 16 and the color to **Dark Gray**.

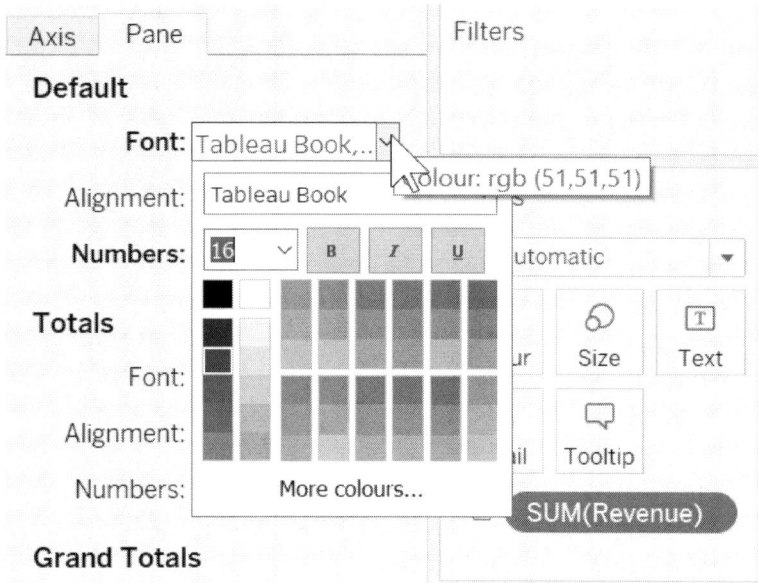

11. Go to **Alignment**, and set the Horizontal alignment to **Center**, and the Vertical alignment to **Middle**.

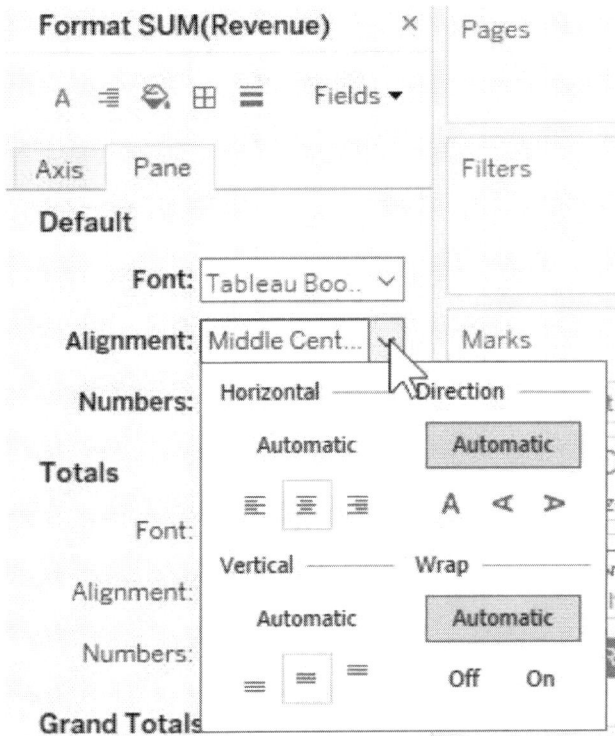

12. Go to the **Toolbar**, **Fit**, and select **Entire View**.

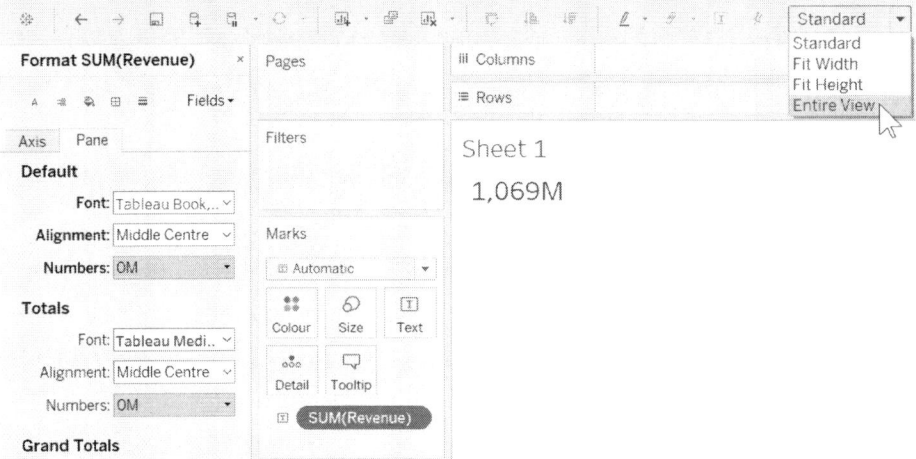

13. Double-click the **Title** Sheet 1 in the canvas to edit it.

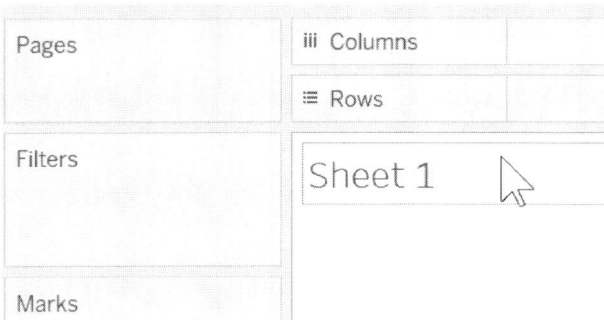

14. Change the title to **Revenue** and click on **Center** alignment and click **OK**.

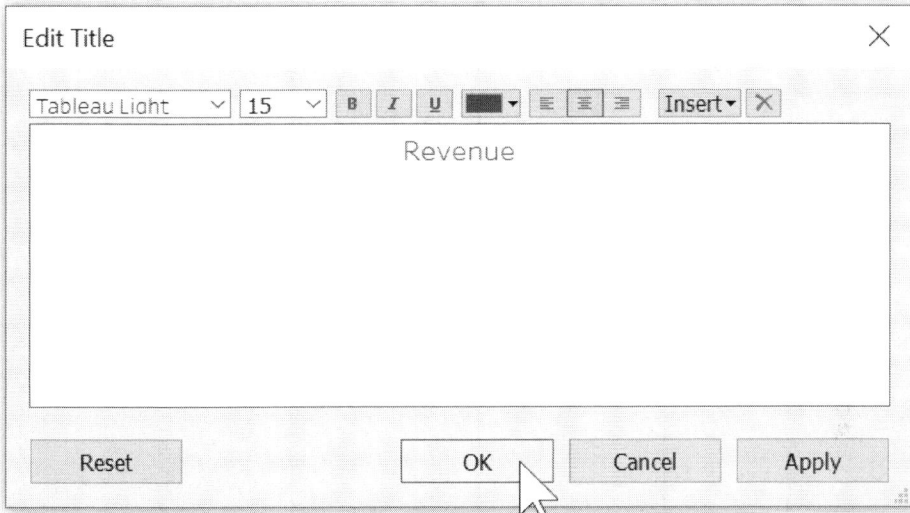

15. Go to the **Marks** card and click on **Size**.

16. Move the **Slider** to the second mark. This slider makes the mark bigger or smaller.

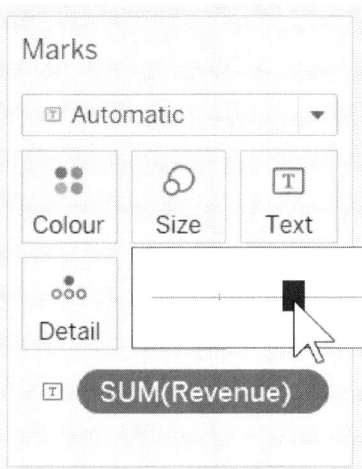

17. Right-click the **Sheet 1** tab and click on **Rename**.

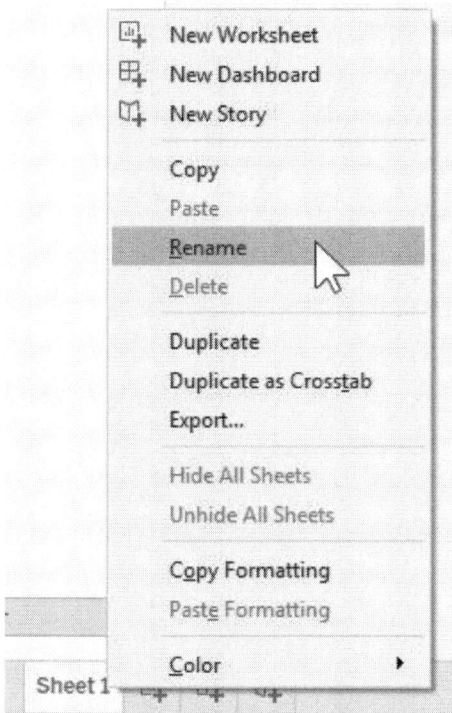

18. Change the sheet name to **Revenue**.

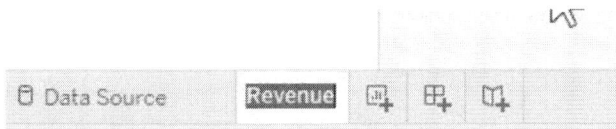

Data Source | Revenue

6. Total Cost

1. Go to the sheet tab bar and click on **New Worksheet**.

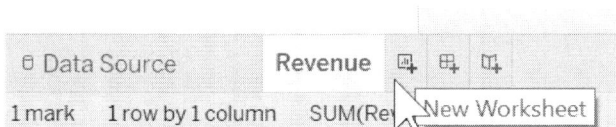

Data Source | Revenue

1 mark   1 row by 1 column   SUM(Re) New Worksheet

2. Double-click the **Sheet 2** name to edit the name.

Data Source | Revenue | Sheet 2

3. Type the name **Total Cost** and hit Enter or click on the canvas.

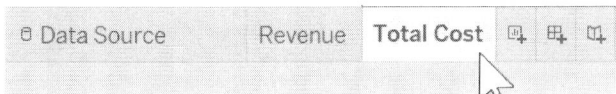

Data Source | Revenue | Total Cost

4. Go Data pane and click on **Total Cost**.

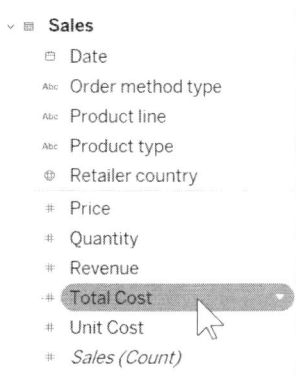

- ⊞ **Sales**
  - Date
  - Abc Order method type
  - Abc Product line
  - Abc Product type
  - ⊕ Retailer country
  - # Price
  - # Quantity
  - # Revenue
  - # Total Cost
  - # Unit Cost
  - # Sales (Count)

5. Drag the **Total Cost** measure from the data pane and drop it on **Marks** as the image below.

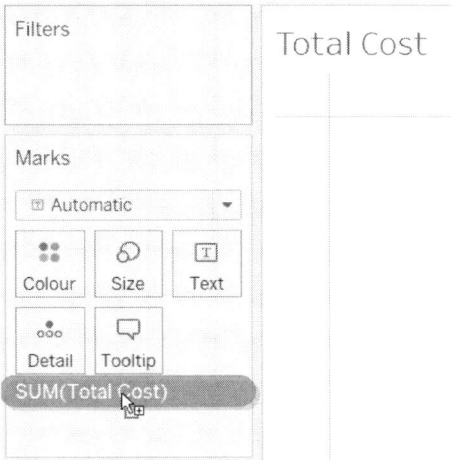

Filters	Total Cost

Marks

⊡ Automatic ▾

Colour	Size	Text

Detail	Tooltip

SUM(Total Cost)

7. Click on the left icon and select **Text**.

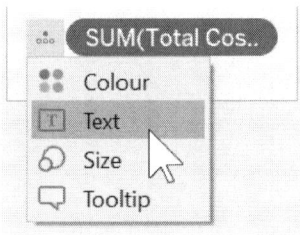

SUM(Total Cos..

- Colour
- Text
- Size
- Tooltip

8. Click on the **down arrow** inside the Total Cost pill. Then click on **Format**.

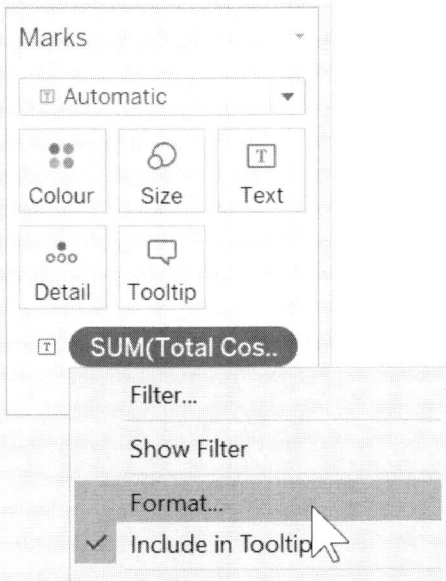

9. Go to the sidebar on the left and click on **Pane** tab.

10. Go to **Default**, **Numbers**, and click on **Number Custom**. Then, set the decimal places to **Zero** and change the **Display Units** to **Millions (M)**.

Format SUM(Total Cost)	×	Pages		iii Columns
A ≡ ≡ ⊞ ≡ Fields ▾				≡ Rows

Axis	Pane		Filters	Total Cost
Default				617,796,671

Font: Tableau Book,.. ▾

Alignment: Automatic ▾   Marks

Numbers: 123,456 ▾   ⊡ Automatic ▾

	Automatic	Number (Custom)
Totals	Number (Standard)	Decimal places:
	Number (Custom)	0 ⬍
Font:	Currency (Standard)	Negative values:
	Currency (Custom)	-1234 ▾
Alignment:	Scientific	Display Units:
	Percentage	None ▾
Numbers:	Custom	None
		Thousands (K)
Grand Total		Millions (M)
		Billions (B) ds separators
Font:		Billions (G)

11. Go to **Default**, **Font**, and change the **Font Size** to 16 and the color to **Dark Gray**.

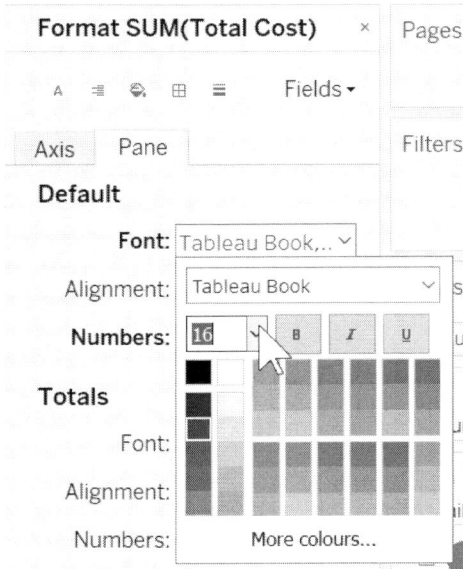

12. Go to **Alignment**, and set the Horizontal alignment to **Center**, and the Vertical alignment to **Middle**.

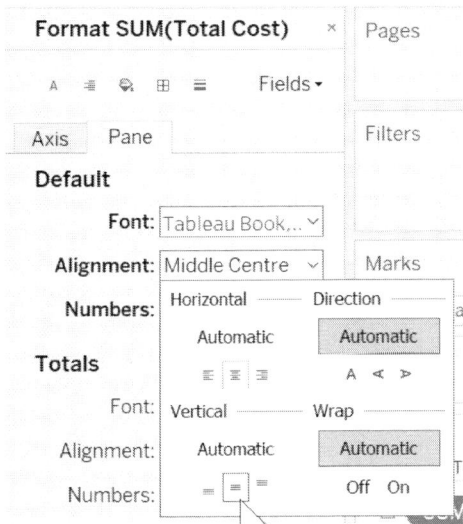

13. Go to the **Toolbar**, **Fit,** and select **Entire View**.

14. Double-click the **Title** in the canvas to edit it.

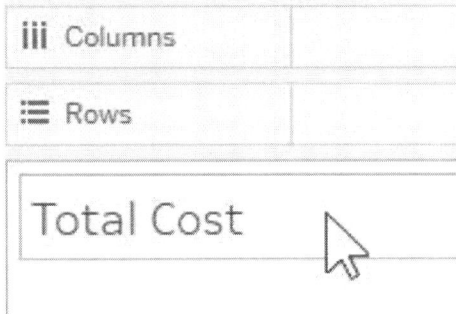

15. Select **Center** alignment and click **OK**. You don't need to change title, once the "Sheet Name" is what we need.

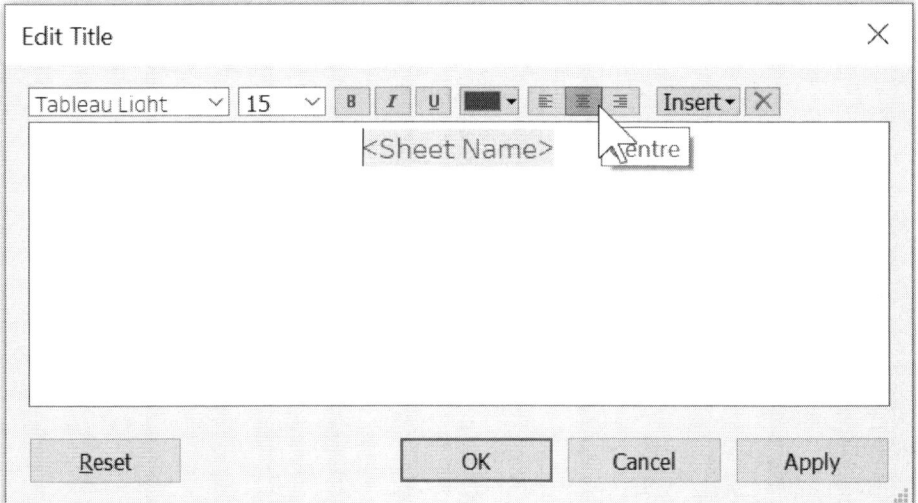

16. Go to the **Marks** card and click on **Size**. Then Move the **Slider** to the second mark.

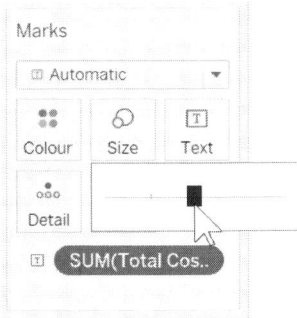

7. Gross Margin

1. Go to the sheet tab bar and click on **New Worksheet**. Then Double-click the tab name to edit the name, type **Gross Margin** and hit **Enter** or click on the canvas.

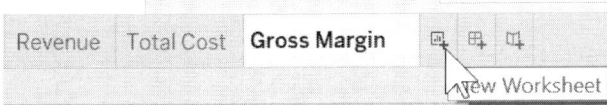

2. Go to **Data pane**, drag **Gross Margin,** and drop it on the **Text** area in the **Marks** as the image below.

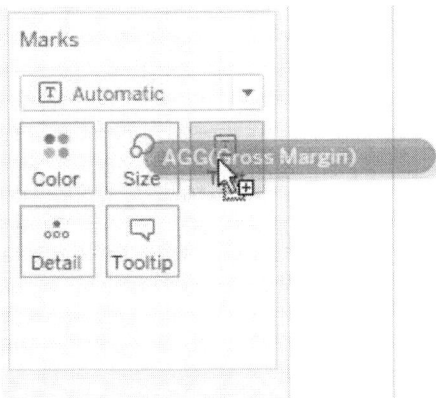

3. Click on the **down arrow** inside the Gross Margin pill. Then click on **Format**.

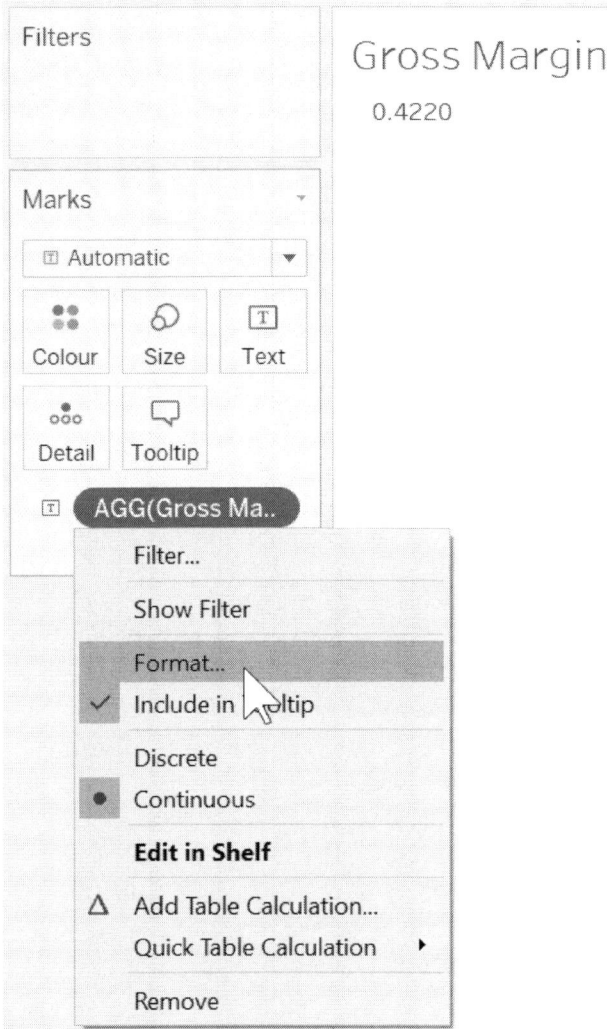

4. Go to the sidebar on the left and click on **Pane** tab. Then go to **Default**, **Numbers**, and click on **Percentage**. Then, set the decimal places to Zero.

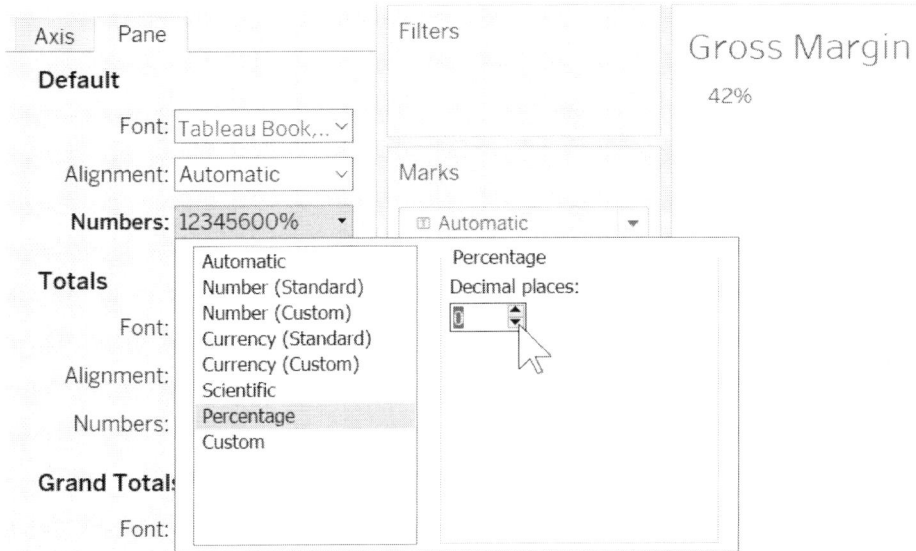

5. Go to **Default**, **Font**, and change the **Font Size** to 16 and the color to **Dark Gray**.

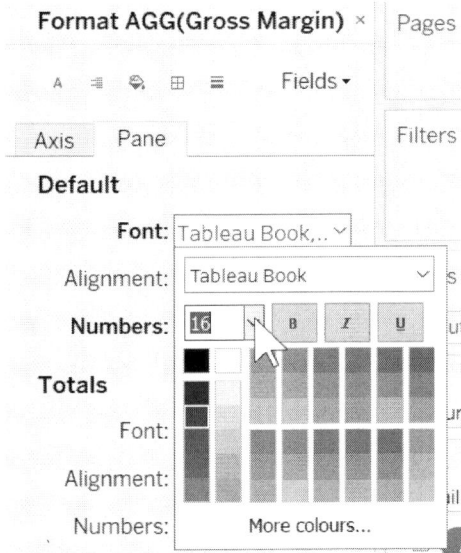

6. Go to **Alignment**, and set the Horizontal alignment to **Center**, and the Vertical alignment to **Middle**.

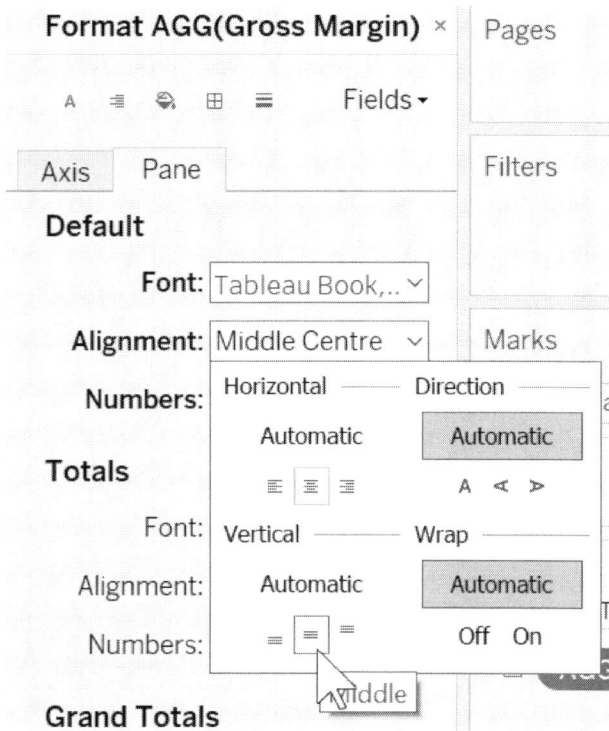

7. Go to the **Toolbar**, **Fit,** and select **Entire View**.

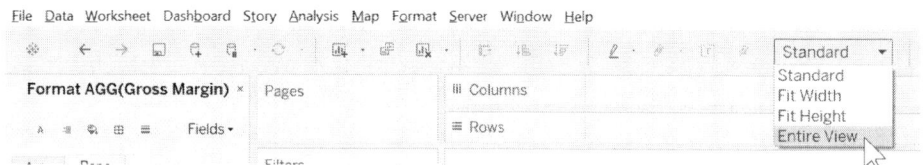

8. Right-click the **Title** in the canvas and click o **Edit Tile**.

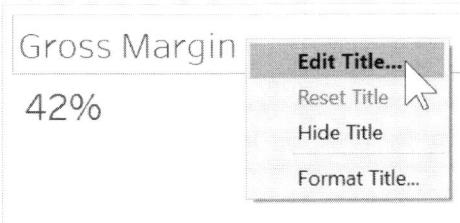

Gross Margin

42%

Edit Title...

Reset Title

Hide Title

Format Title...

9. Select **Center** alignment and click **OK**.

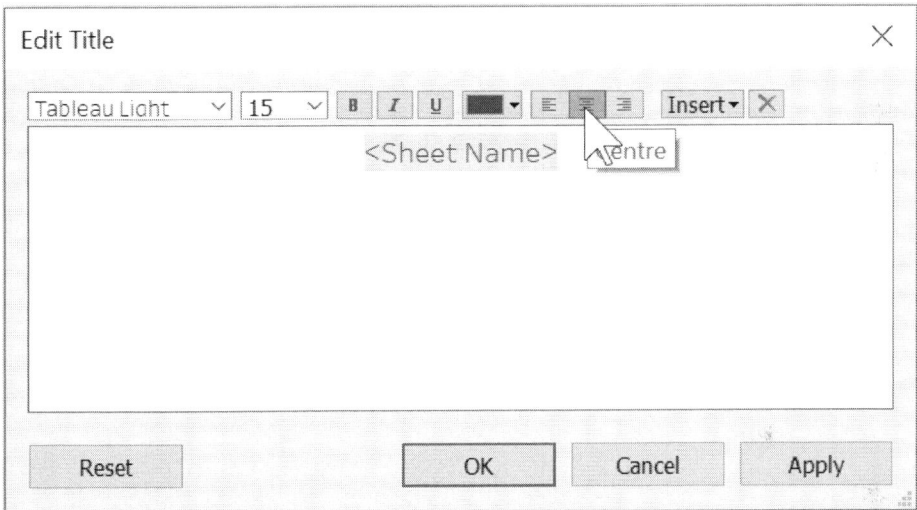

Edit Title ✕

Tableau Light ▾ 15 ▾ **B** *I* U ■ ▾ ≡ ≡ ≡ Insert ▾ ✕

\<Sheet Name\> Centre

Reset 　　OK 　　Cancel 　　Apply

10. Go to the **Marks** card and click on **Size**. Then Move the **Slider** to the second mark.

Marks

Automatic ▾

Colour　Size　Text

Detail

AGG(Gross Ma..

8. Bar Chart - Revenue by Year

Vertical bar charts are best for comparing data across categories is works fine when you don't have too many groups (no more than 12 is usually good). Each bar is separated by blank space, indicating no inherent order to your groups. The point values can be compared between themselves or values inside the category.

1. Go to the sheet tab bar and click on **New Worksheet**. Then Double-click the tab name to edit it; type **Revenue by Year** and hit **Enter** or click on the canvas.

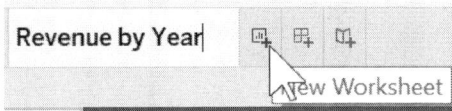

2. Go to Data pane and drag the **Revenue** field to the **Rows** shelf.

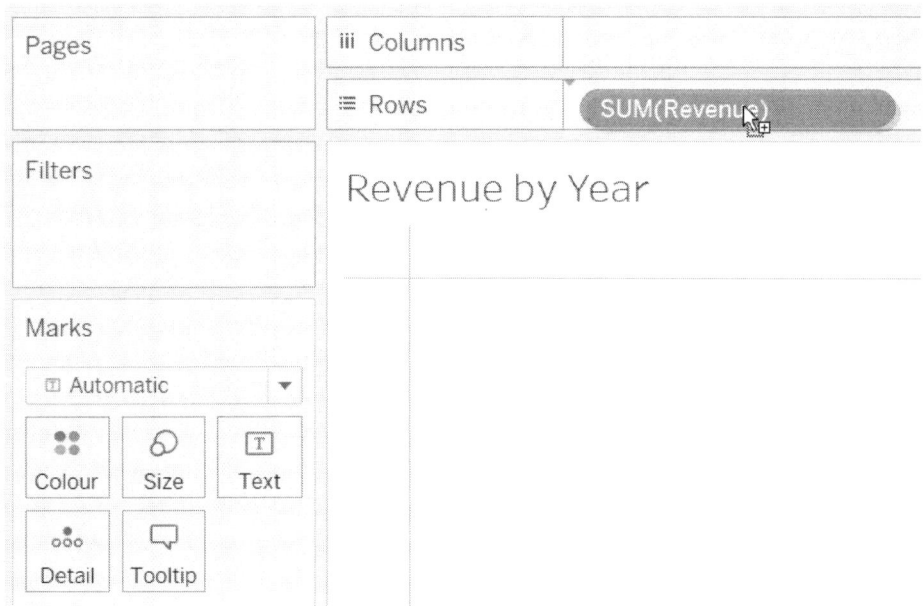

3. Go to Data pane and drag the **Full Date** field to the **Columns** shelf.

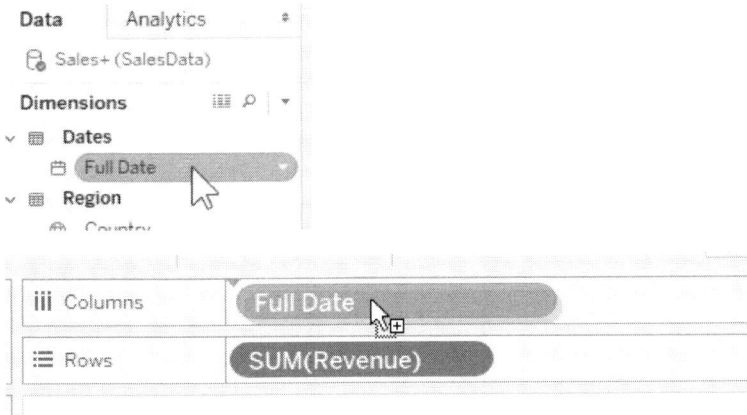

| Data | Analytics | ⬦ |

🔒 Sales+ (SalesData)

Dimensions

∨ ▦ **Dates**
    📅 Full Date
∨ ▦ **Region**
    ⊕ Country

| ⠿ Columns | Full Date |
| ☰ Rows | SUM(Revenue) |

4. Go to the **Marks** card, click the **Mark Type** drop-down, and select **Bar**.

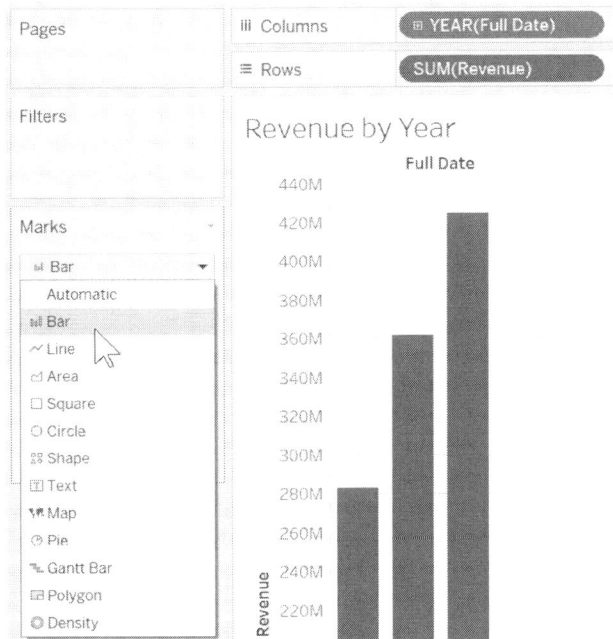

Pages

| ⠿ Columns | ⊞ YEAR(Full Date) |
| ☰ Rows | SUM(Revenue) |

Filters

Marks

⊪ Bar ▾
   Automatic
   ⊪ Bar
   ∿ Line
   ⊿ Area
   ◻ Square
   ○ Circle
   ⁂ Shape
   ⊞ Text
   ▼ Map
   ⊙ Pie
   ⅂ Gantt Bar
   ▣ Polygon
   ◐ Density

Revenue by Year

Full Date

440M
420M
400M
380M
360M
340M
320M
300M
280M
260M
240M
220M

Revenue

5. Also, drag the **Full Date** field to the **Filters** shelf.

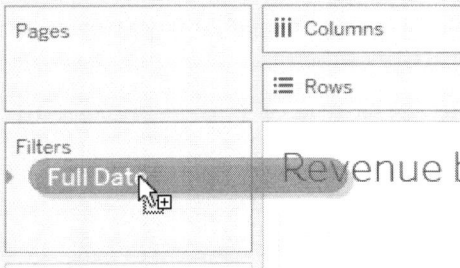

| Pages | iii Columns |
| | ≡ Rows |

| Filters | |
| ► Full Date | Revenue t |

6. A **Filter Field** window will appear. Select the option **Year** to filter the chart by a specific year. Then, click **Next**

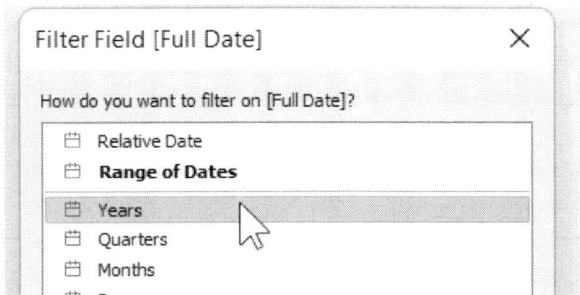

Filter Field [Full Date]   ✕

How do you want to filter on [Full Date]?

📅 Relative Date
📅 **Range of Dates**
📅 Years
📅 Quarters
📅 Months

7. We need this report to show data from **2016 to 2018**. Check the boxes whithin this period. Then, click **OK**.

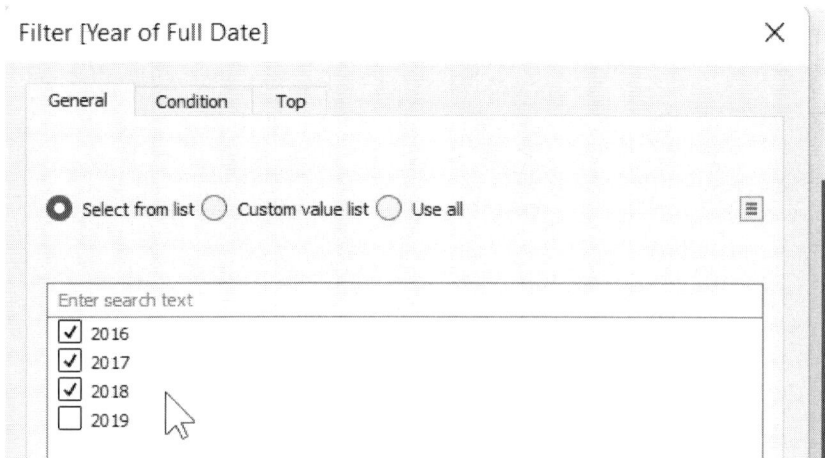

Filter [Year of Full Date]   ✕

General   Condition   Top

⦿ Select from list ◯ Custom value list ◯ Use all   ▤

Enter search text

☑ 2016
☑ 2017
☑ 2018
☐ 2019

8. Your chart should look like the image below.

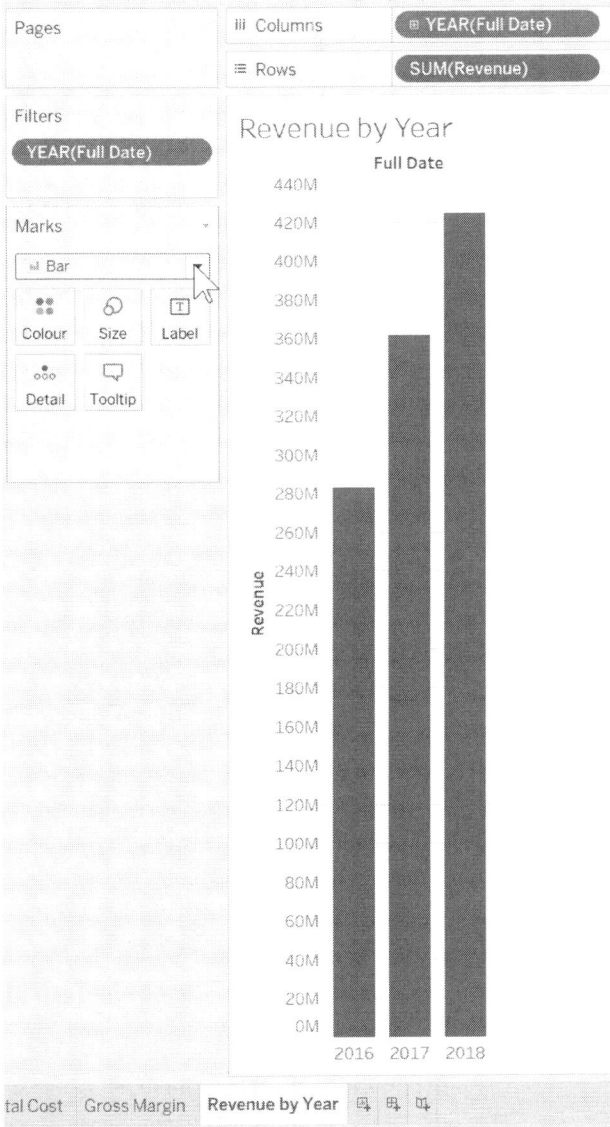

9. Go to the **Toolbar**, **Fit,** and select **Entire View**.

10. The chart view has changed. It is spread across the canvas.

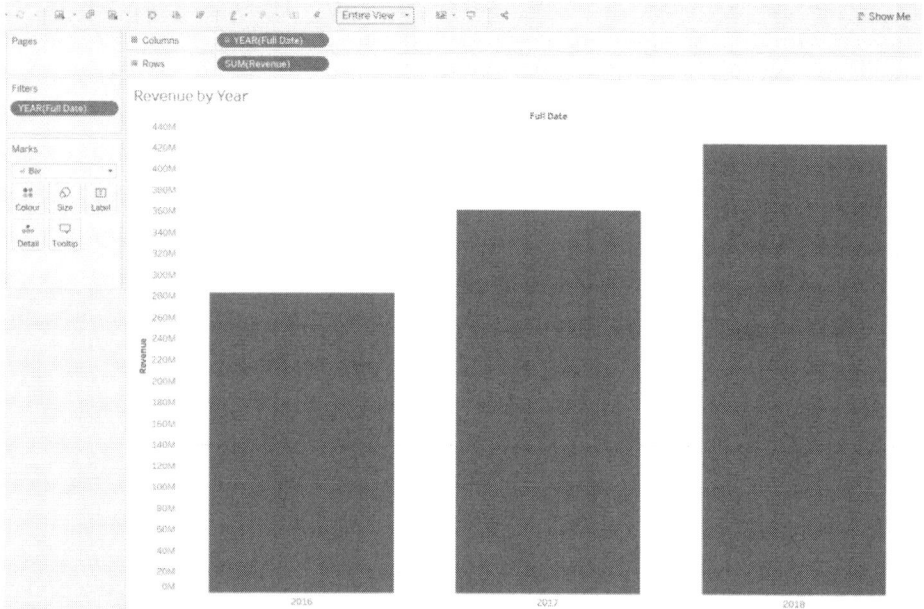

11. Go to **Marks** and click on **Label**, check the option **Show mark labels**.

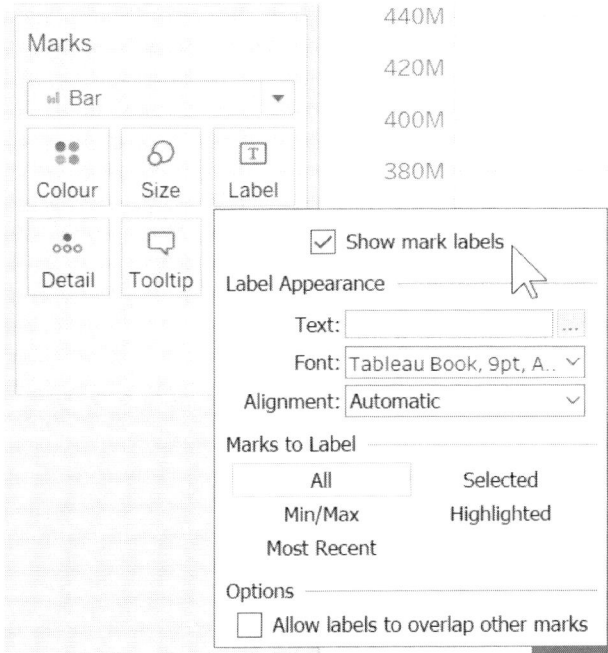

Marks	440M
	420M
Bar ▼	400M
	380M

Colour   Size   Label

Detail   Tooltip

☑ Show mark labels

Label Appearance

Text: [   ] [...]

Font: [Tableau Book, 9pt, A.. ▼]

Alignment: [Automatic   ▼]

Marks to Label

All	Selected
Min/Max	Highlighted
Most Recent	

Options

☐ Allow labels to overlap other marks

12. Go to the **Rows** shelf and click on the down arrow inside the **Revenue** pill. Then click on **Format**.

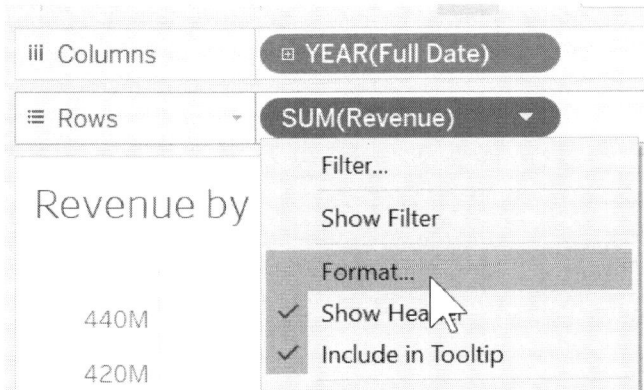

iii Columns   ⊞ YEAR(Full Date)

≡ Rows   ▼   SUM(Revenue)   ▼

Revenue by

Filter...

Show Filter

Format...

✓ Show Hea...

✓ Include in Tooltip

440M

420M

13. Go to the sidebar on the left and click on **Pane** tab. Go to **Default**, **Numbers**, and click on **Number Custom**. Then, set the decimal places to Zero and change the **Display Units** to Millions (M).

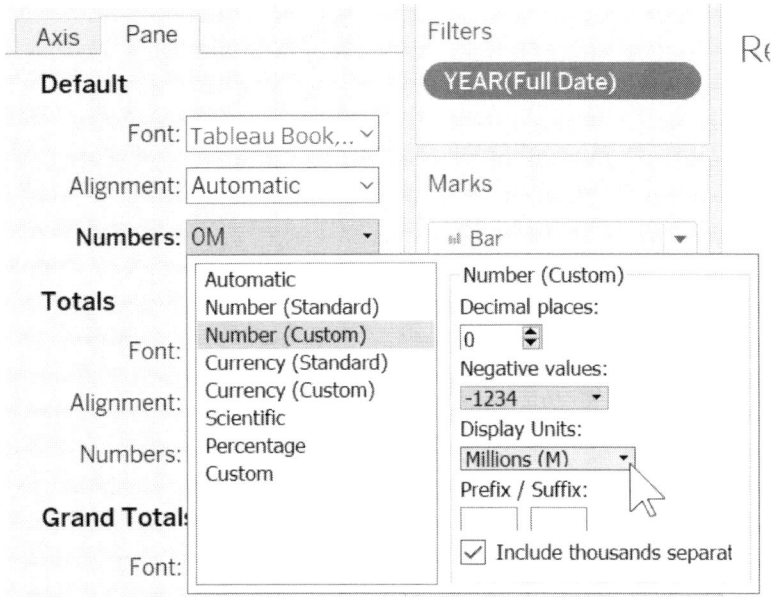

14. Go to the **Marks**, **Color**, and click on **More Colors** to change the color of the chart.

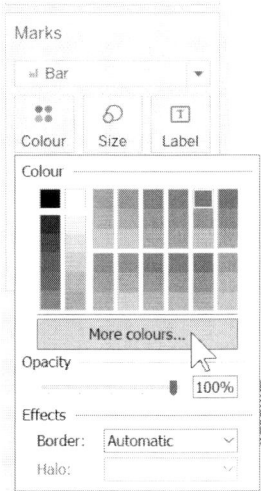

15. Go to **HTML** text box and type the color code **#49525e** . Then click, **OK**.

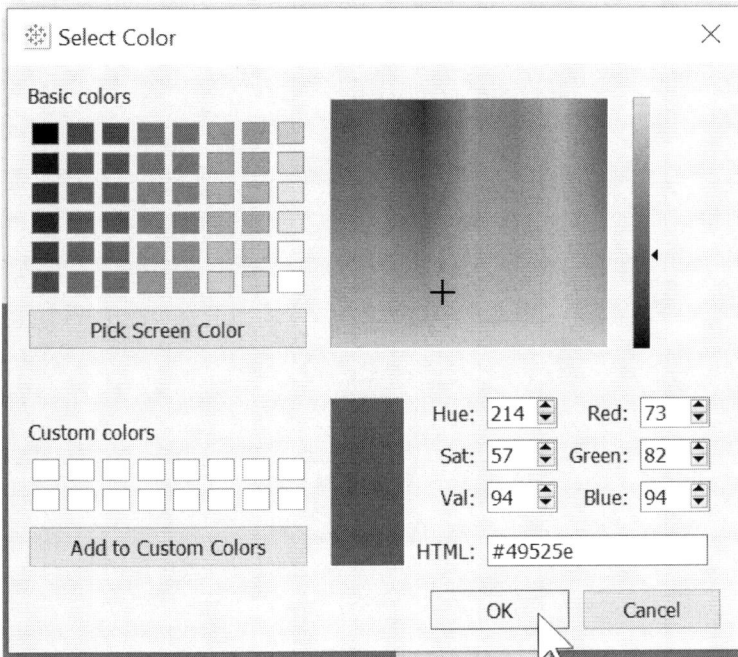

16. Right-click the vertical axis and uncheck the option **Show Header**.

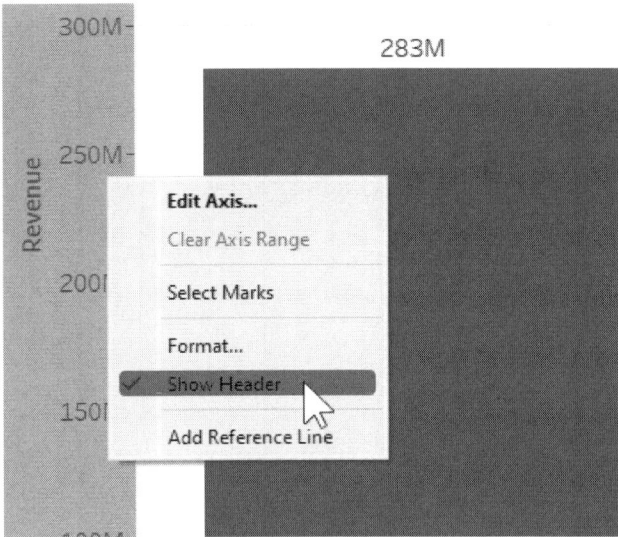

17. Right-click the Full Date label and select Hide Field Labels for Columns.

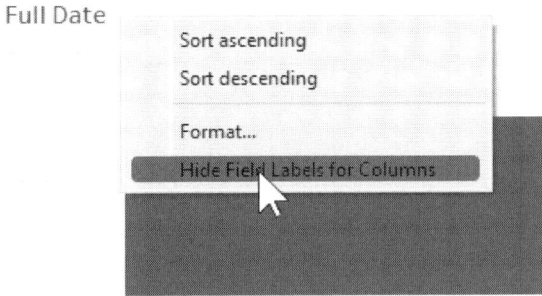

18. The chart should look like the image below.

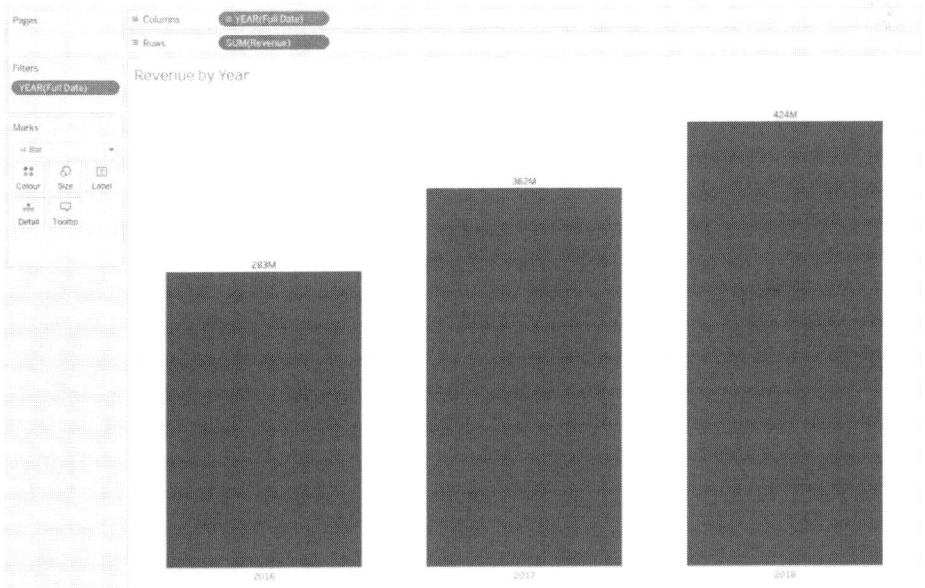

9. Pie Chart - Revenue by Order Method

The Pie Chart is essentially a circle divided into sectors; it is easy to read and make a good choice if you want to show proportions of a whole. A Doughnut Chart variant of the pie chart, with a blank center allowing for additional information about the data as a whole to be included.

An arc specifies each point that length is proportional to the circumference as the data value to the total sum of all values.

1. Go to the sheet tab bar and click on **New Worksheet**. Double-click the tab name to edit it; type **Revenue by Order** and hit **Enter** or click on the canvas.

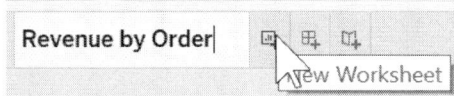

Revenue by Order|

New Worksheet

2. Drag the **Revenue** from the data pane and drop it on **Marks** as in the image below.

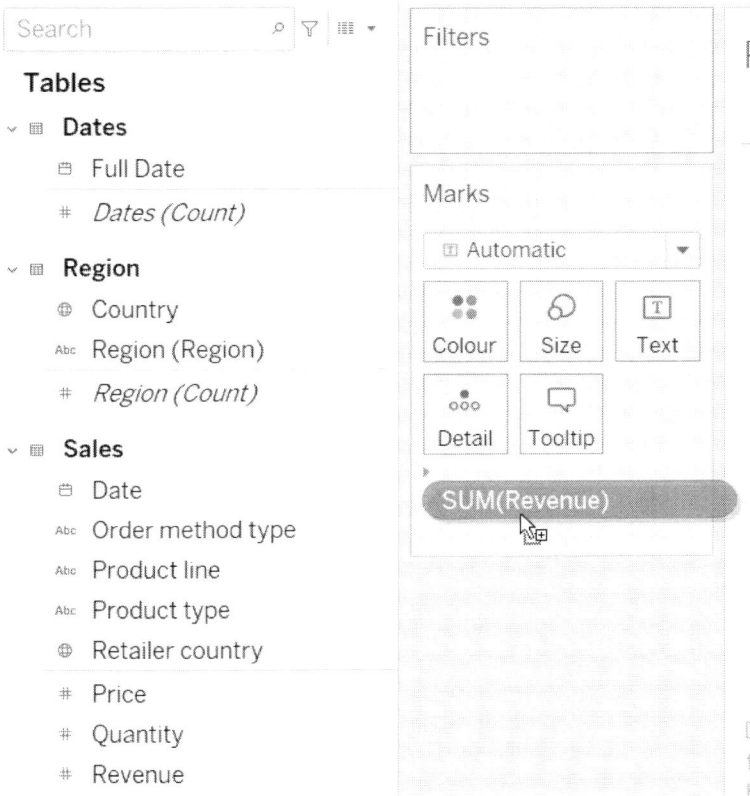

Search	⚲ ▽ ▦ ▾

Tables

⌄ ▦ **Dates**

   🗓 Full Date

   # *Dates (Count)*

⌄ ▦ **Region**

   ⊕ Country

   Abc Region (Region)

   # *Region (Count)*

⌄ ▦ **Sales**

   🗓 Date

   Abc Order method type

   Abc Product line

   Abc Product type

   ⊕ Retailer country

   # Price

   # Quantity

   # Revenue

Filters

Marks

▦ Automatic ▾

Colour	Size	Text

Detail	Tooltip

SUM(Revenue)

3. Click on the left icon and select **Text**.

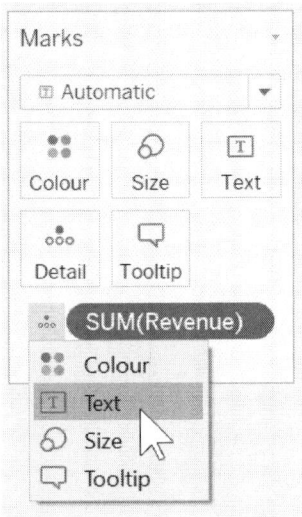

4. Go to Data pane and drag the **Order method type** field to the **Marks** card.

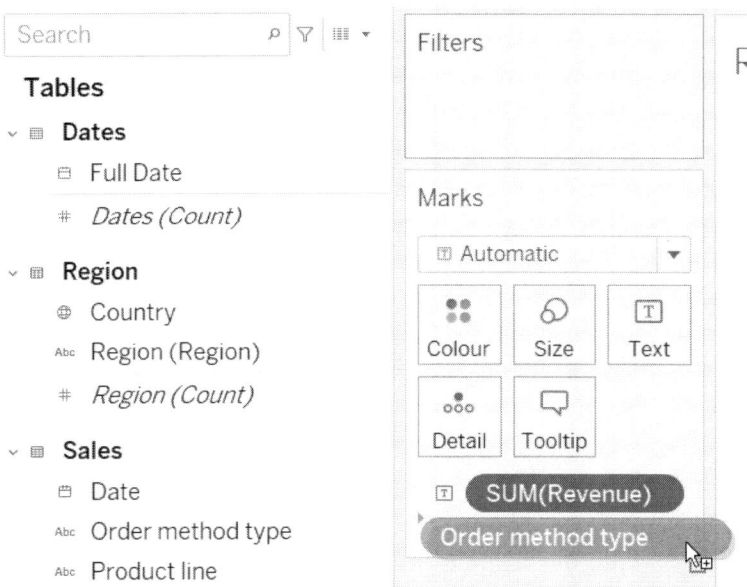

5. At the right side of the screen, go to **Show Me** area. You can click on the button to show or hide the chart and graphs option.

6. Select the **Pie Chart**.

7. Tableau will adapt the **Marks** items according to the Pie chart structure.

8. Again, drag the **Revenue** from the data pane and drop it on **Marks** as in the image below.

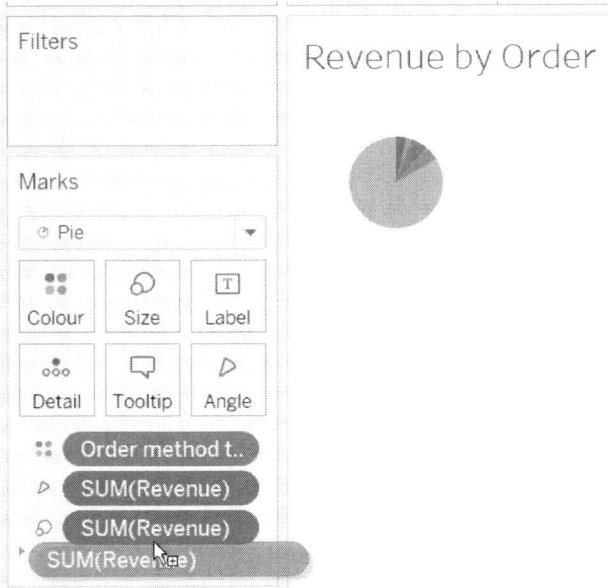

9. Click on the left icon and select **Label** as the image below.

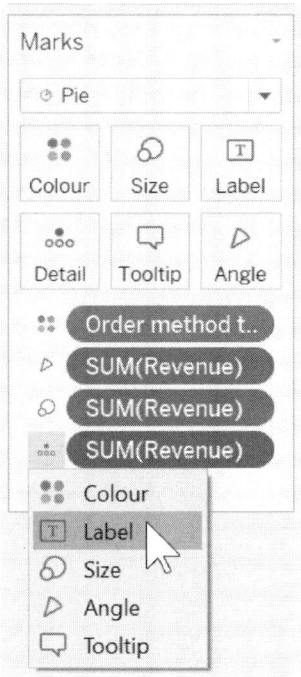

10. Click on the **down arrow** inside the **Revenue** pill. Then click on **Format**.

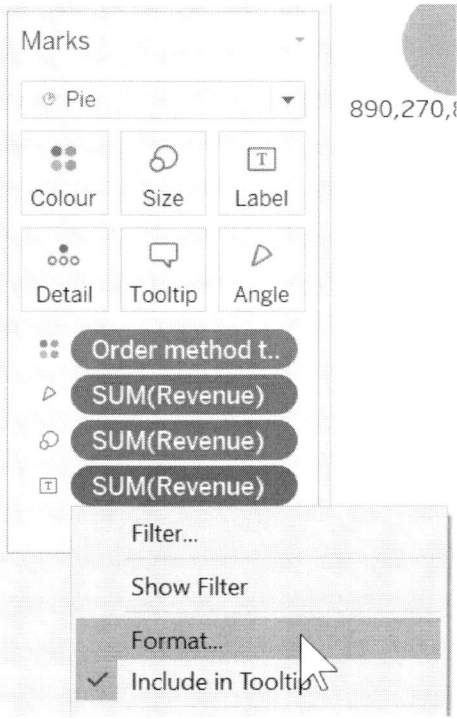

11. Go to the sidebar on the left and click on **Pane** tab. Then go to **Default**, **Numbers**, and click on **Number Custom**. Then, set the decimal places to **Zero** and change the **Display Units** to **Millions (M)**.

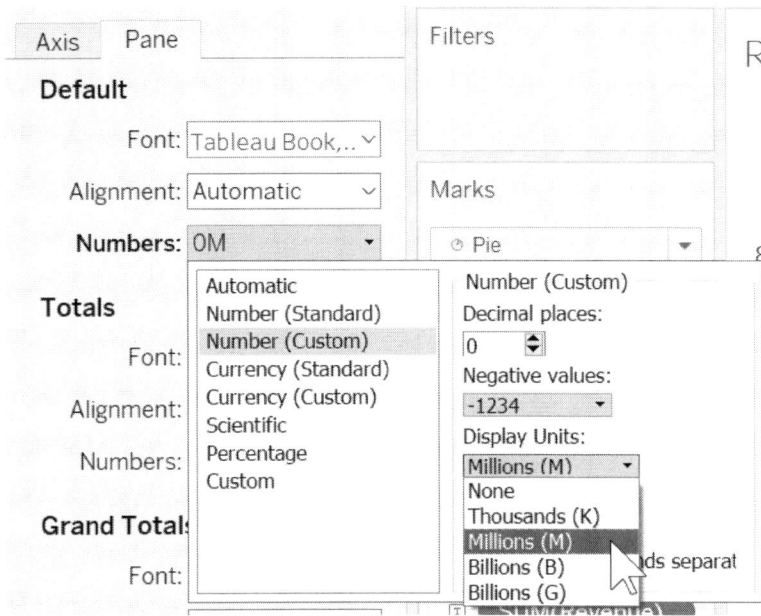

12. Go to the **Toolbar**, **Fit,** and select **Entire View**.

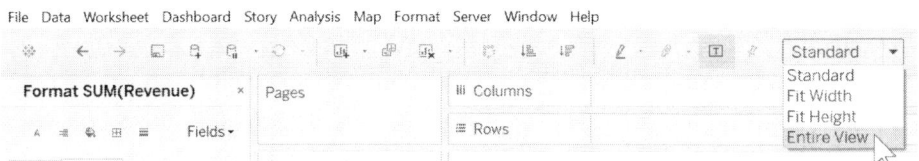

13. Go to the **Marks**, **Color**, and click on **Edit Colors** to change the color of the chart.

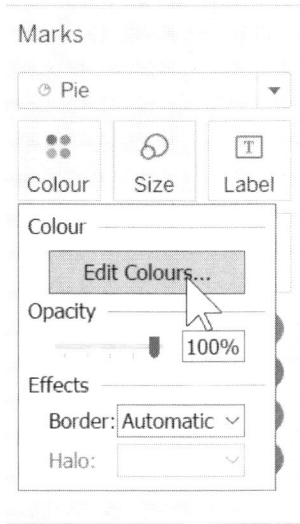

Marks

| ⊙ Pie | ▼ |

⠐⠂	⬭	T
Colour	Size	Label

Colour

Edit Colours...

Opacity

100%

Effects

Border: Automatic ∨

Halo: ∨

14. Go to Select Color Palette and select Jewel Bright or Summer.

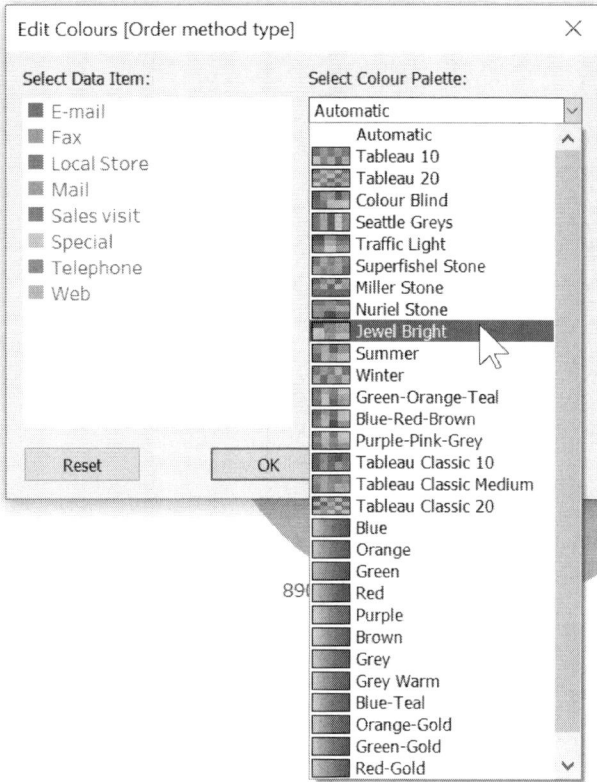

Edit Colours [Order method type]   ✕

Select Data Item: Select Colour Palette:

■ E-mail | Automatic |▽|
■ Fax   Automatic   ⌃
■ Local Store   Tableau 10
■ Mail   Tableau 20
■ Sales visit   Colour Blind
▨ Special   Seattle Greys
■ Telephone   Traffic Light
▨ Web   Superfishel Stone
                                           Miller Stone
                                           Nuriel Stone
                                           Jewel Bright
                                           Summer
                                           Winter
                                           Green-Orange-Teal
                                           Blue-Red-Brown
       Reset   OK   Purple-Pink-Grey
                                           Tableau Classic 10
                                           Tableau Classic Medium
                                           Tableau Classic 20
                              89(Blue
                                           Orange
                                           Green
                                           Red
                                           Purple
                                           Brown
                                           Grey
                                           Grey Warm
                                           Blue-Teal
                                           Orange-Gold
                                           Green-Gold
                                           Red-Gold   ⌄

15. Click on Assign Palette.

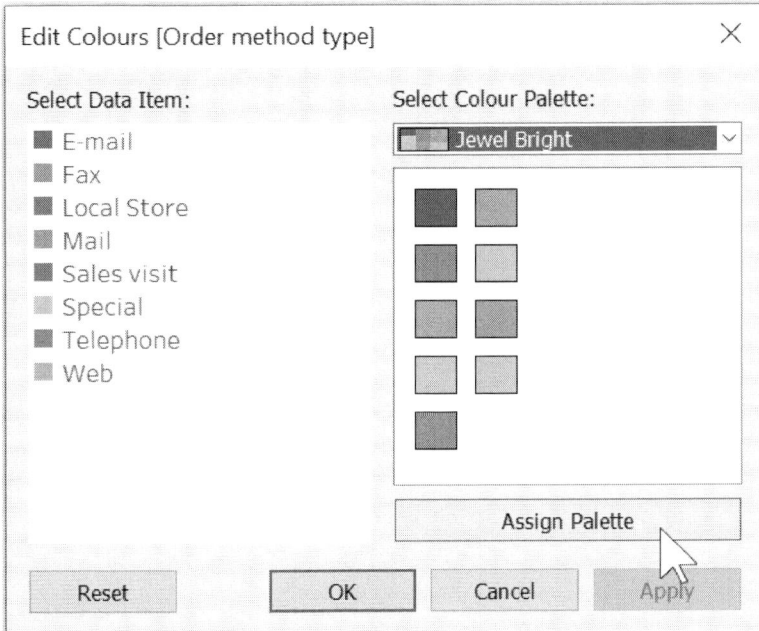

Edit Colours [Order method type]   ✕

Select Data Item: Select Colour Palette:

■ E-mail   ▢▢ Jewel Bright   ⌄
■ Fax
■ Local Store
■ Mail
■ Sales visit
■ Special
■ Telephone
■ Web

                                                 Assign Palette

  Reset   OK   Cancel   Apply

16. Tableau can change the color order. If you want to change the color, just select the item on the left side and change the color on the right side. In this example, I selected the **Web** and changed to **Green.**

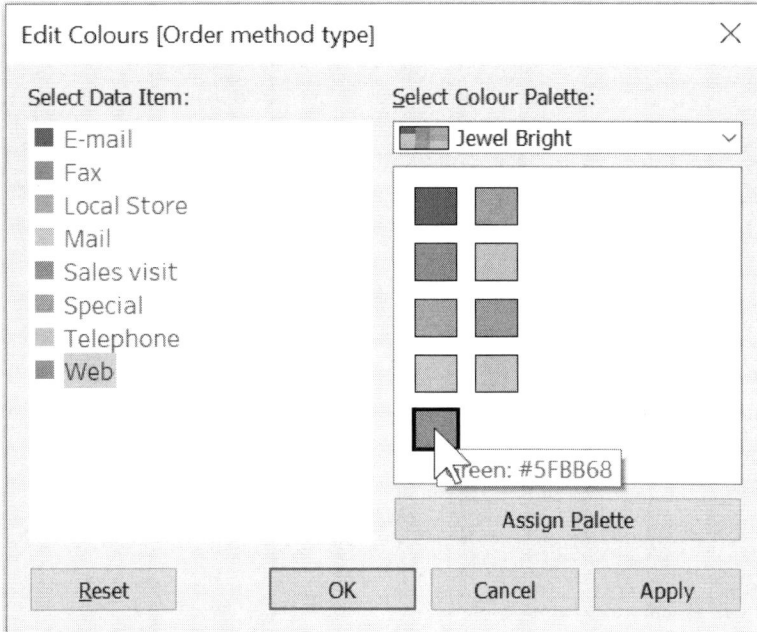

17. Then, I selected **Sales visit** and changed to **Light Blue**. To leave the window, click, **OK**.

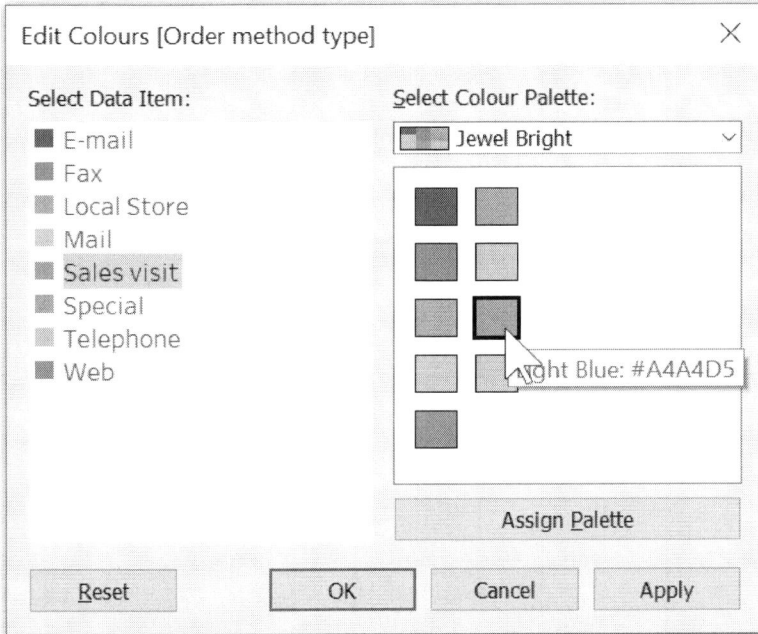

18. Click on **Color** and change the **Opacity** to **70%**.

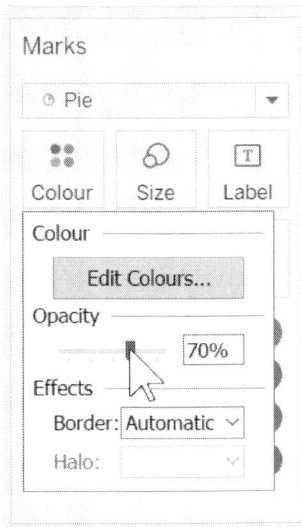

19. The Pie chart should look like the image below.

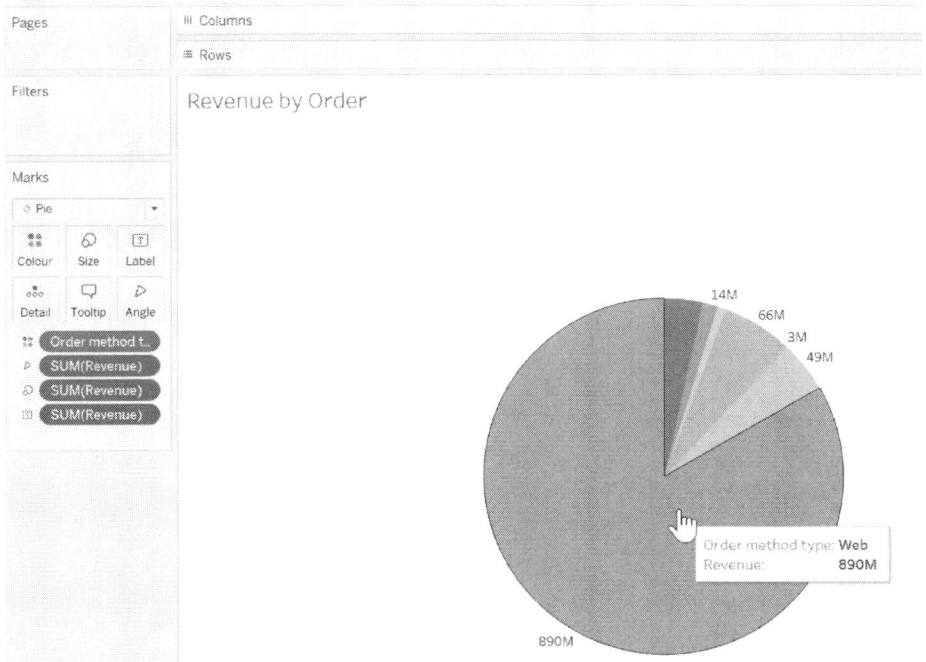

10. Treemap - Revenue by Product Line

Treemaps are a relatively simple data visualization that can provide insight in a visually attractive format. This chart is intended for the visualization of hierarchical data in the form of nested rectangles. Each level is often called a branch containing other rectangles (leaves).

1. Go to the sheet tab bar and click on **New Worksheet**. Then Double-click the tab name to edit it; type **Revenue by Product Line** and hit **Enter** or click on the canvas.

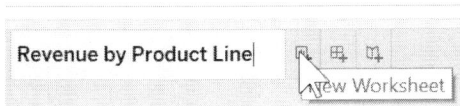

Revenue by Product Line|

New Worksheet

2. Drag the **Revenue** measure from the data pane and drop it on **Marks** as in the image below.

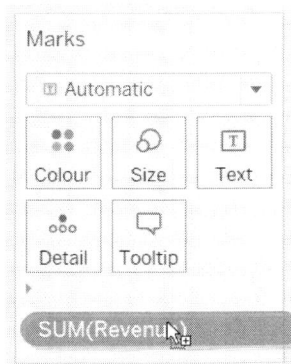

Marks

Automatic

Colour   Size   Text

Detail   Tooltip

SUM(Revenue)

3. Also, drag the fields **Product type**, **Product line,** and again the **Product line**.

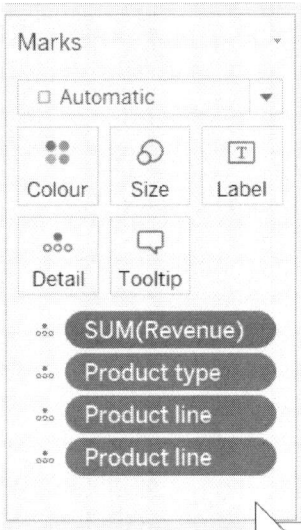

4. Change the **Revenue** pill type to **Size**.

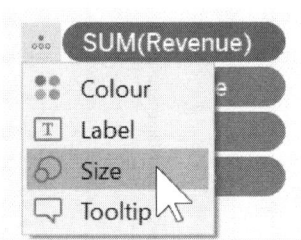

5. Go to **Show Me** and select the **Treemap**.

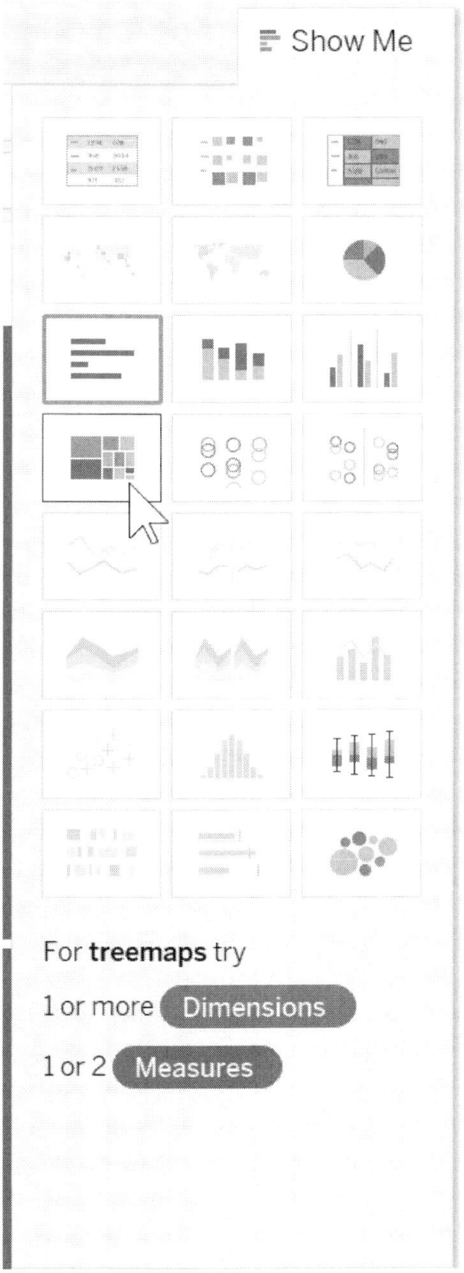

6. If **Tableau** creates any unnecessary pill, click on the down-arrow and click on **Remove**.

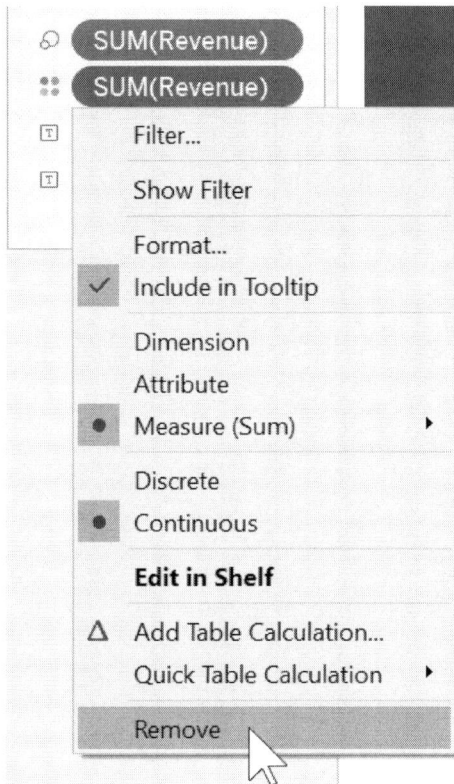

7. Be sure to have the fields **Revenue** (as Size), **Product line** (as Label)**, Product type** (as Label), and **Product line** (as Color).

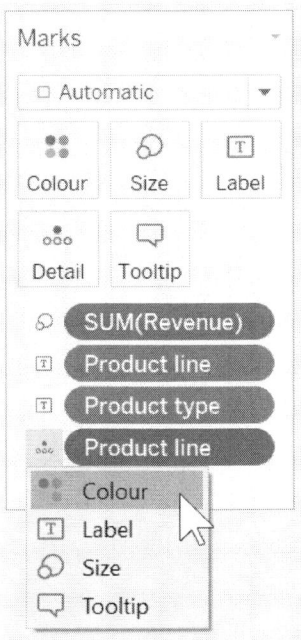

8. Go to the **Toolbar**, **Fit,** and select **Entire View**.

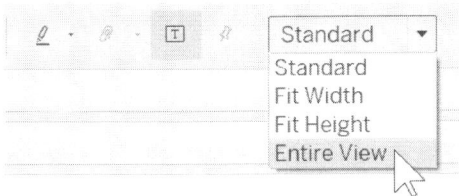

9. Go to **Marks**, click on **Color,** and change the **Opacity** to **85%**.

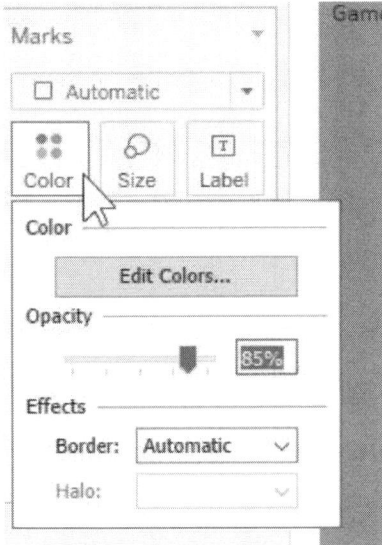

10. The Treemap should look like the image below.

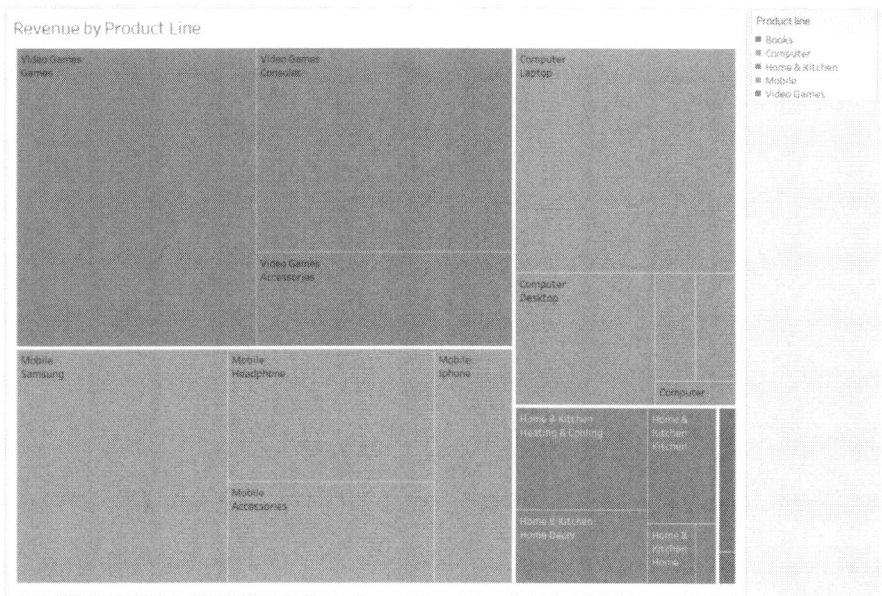

11.   Map - Revenue by Country

Geographic data display geographical regions that are colored, patterned, or shaded in relation to the area. This visual provides a way to show the values over a location. You can work with geographic data by connecting to spatial files or connecting to location data stored in spreadsheets, text files, or on a server.

1. Go to the sheet tab bar and click on **New Worksheet**. Then Double-click the tab name to edit it; type **Revenue by Country** and hit **Enter** or click on the canvas.

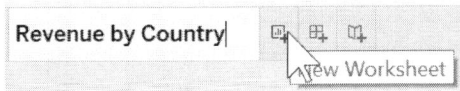

Revenue by Country

New Worksheet

2. Go to Data pane and drag the **Country** field to the **Marks** card.

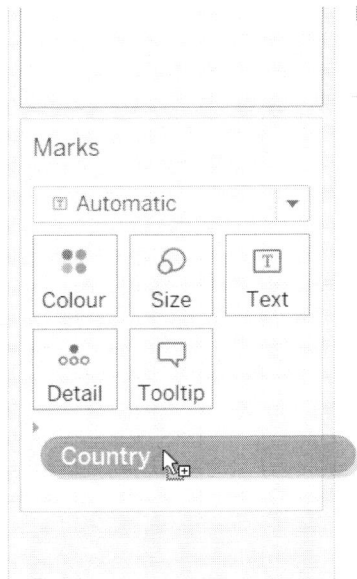

Tables

∨ ▦ **Dates**
   🗓 Full Date
   # *Dates (Count)*

∨ ▦ **Region**
   ⊕ Country
   Abc Region (Region)
   # *Region (Count)*

∨ ▦ **Sales**
   🗓 Date
   Abc Order method type
   Abc Product line
   Abc Product type

Marks

⊡ Automatic ▾

| Colour | Size | Text |
| Detail | Tooltip | |

Country

3. Add the **Region** and **Revenue** fields.

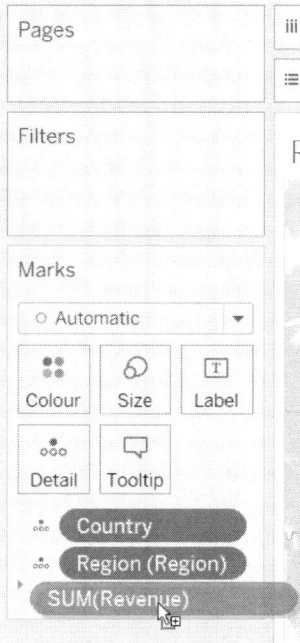

4. Change the **Country** pill to Detail, **Region** to Color, and **Revenue** to Size.

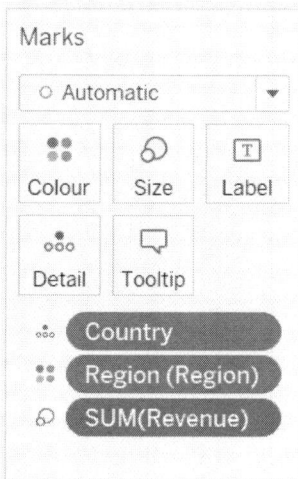

5. Click on **Size**. Then Move the **Slider** to the second mark.

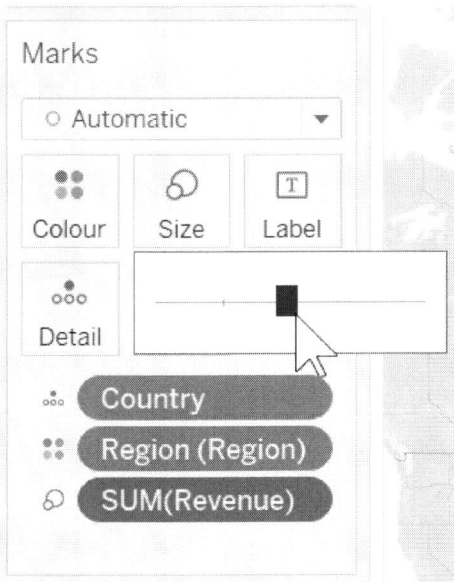

6. Go to **Marks**, click on **Color,** and change the **Opacity** to **85%**.

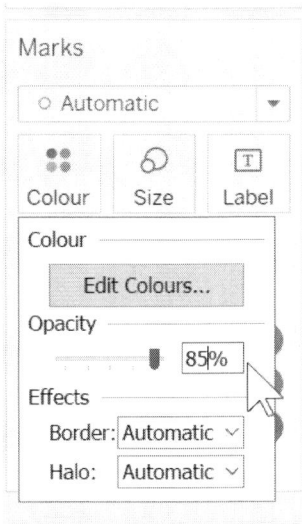

7. The Map should look like the image below.

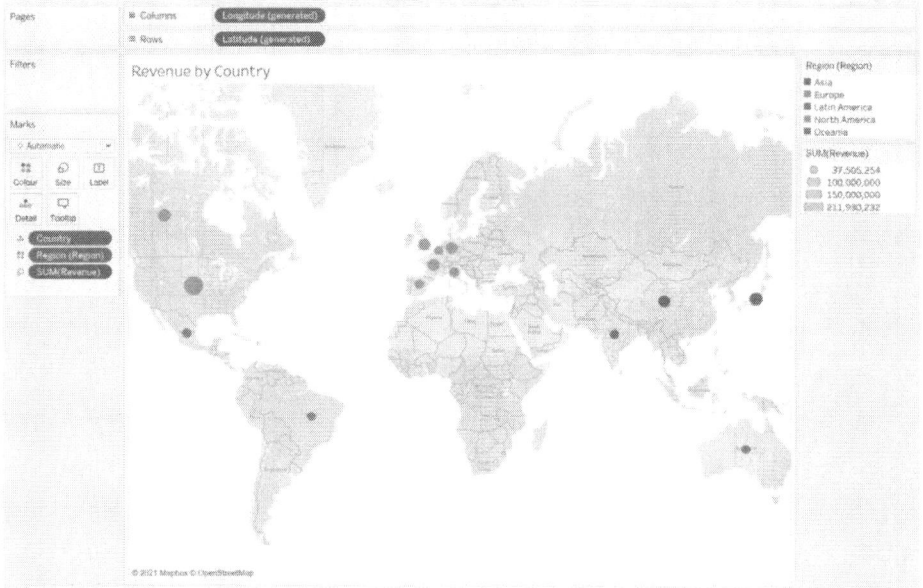

12.   Line Chart - Revenue by Month

Line charts connect individual data points in a view. They provide a simple way to visualize a trend in data over a period of time or a particular correlation. Timeline scale is the most common case for the X-axis of the Chart, but sometimes ordinal scale can also be used.

1. Go to the sheet tab bar and click on **New Worksheet**. Then Double-click the tab name to edit it; type **Revenue by Month** and hit **Enter** or click on the canvas.

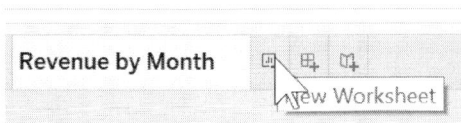

2. Go to Data pane, **Sales**, and drag the **Date** field to the **Columns** shelf.

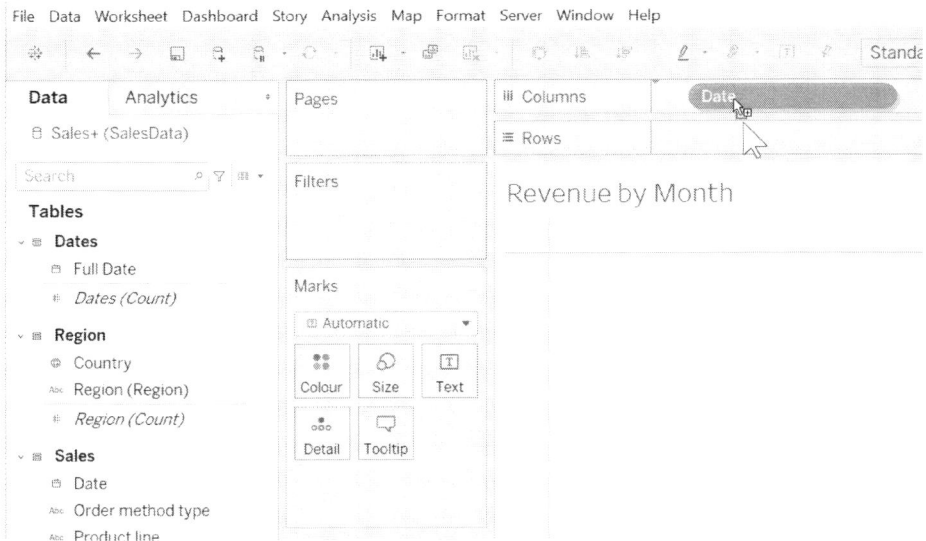

3. Drag the **Revenue** field to the **Rows** shelf.

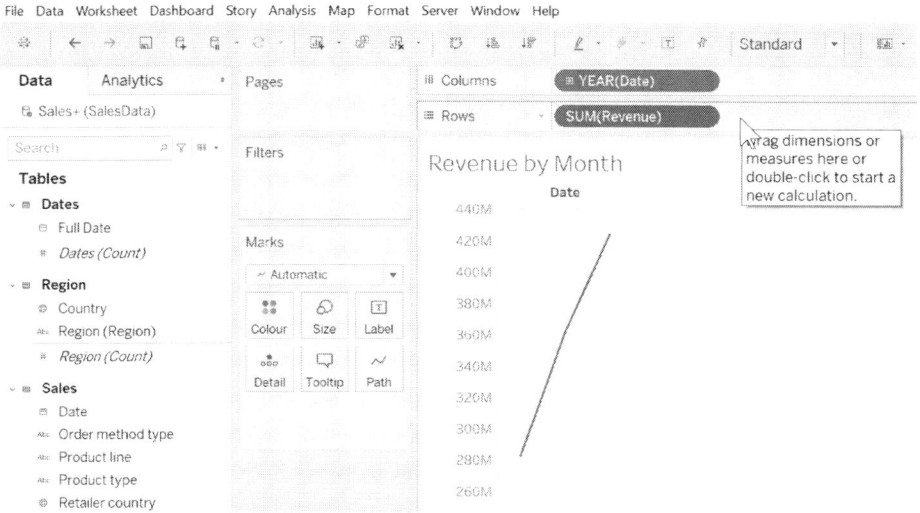

4. Go to the Column shelf and click on the down-arrow of the **Date** pill, and select **Month** (the first one in the selection).

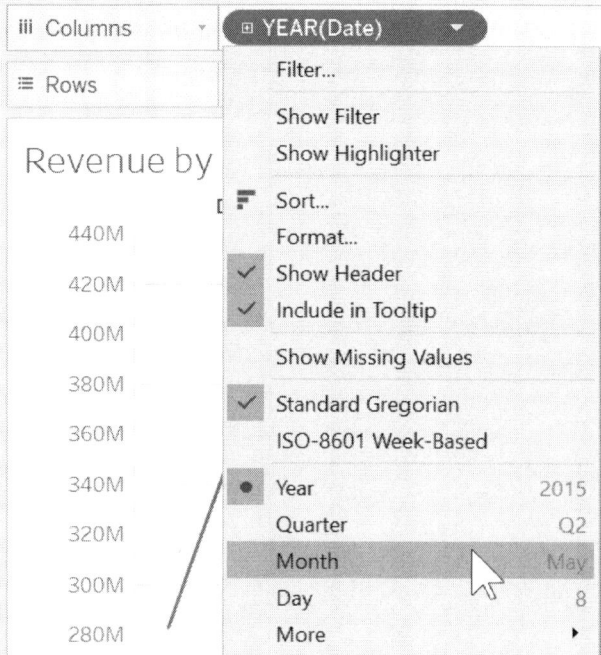

5. Go to Data pane and drag the **Region** and drop it on the **Color** area in the **Marks** as the image below.

Tables

- ⊞ **Dates**
  - ⊟ Full Date
  - ⊹ *Dates (Count)*
- ⊞ **Region**
  - ⊕ Country
  - Abc Region (Region)
  - ⊹ *Region (Count)*
- ⊞ **Sales**
  - ⊟ Date
  - Abc Order method type
  - Abc Product line

Marks

~ Automatic ▼

Region (Region)	🎨	[T]
Colour	Size	Label

⚬⚬⚬	💬	∿
Detail	Tooltip	Path

6. Click on **Size**. Then Move the Slider between the first and second mark.

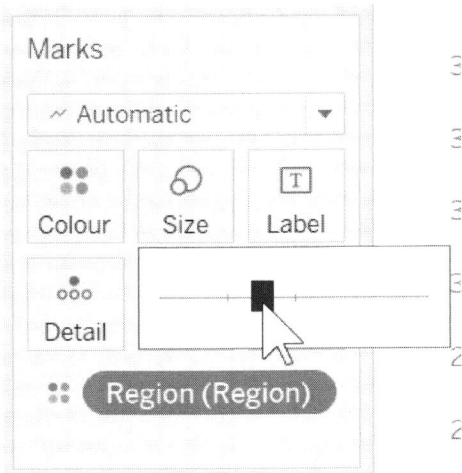

Marks

~ Automatic ▼

⣿	🎨	[T]
Colour	Size	Label

⚬⚬⚬		
Detail		

⣿ Region (Region)

7. Go to **Marks**, click on **Color,** and change the **Opacity** to **85%**.

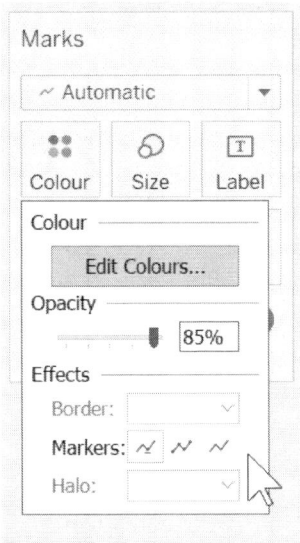

8. Go to the **Toolbar**, **Fit,** and select **Entire View**.

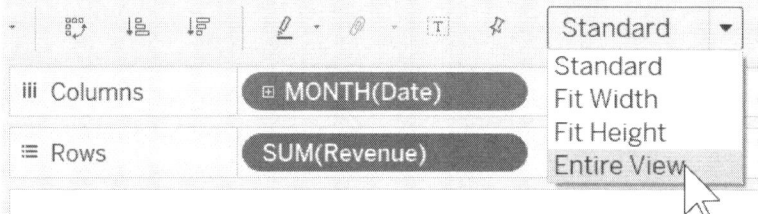

9. The Line Chart should look like the image below.

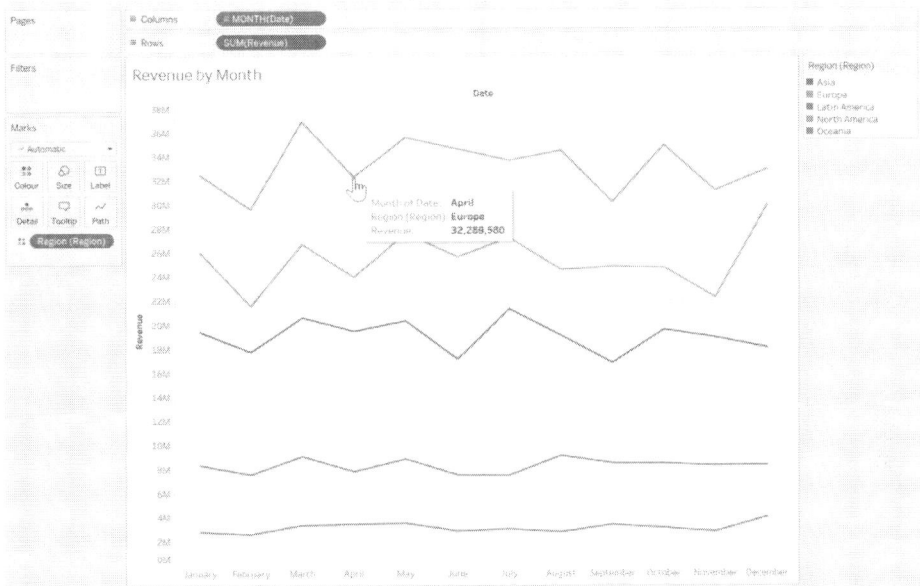

13. Bar Chart - Revenue by Sales Manager

Horizontal bar charts are similar to a vertical bar chart and are typically used with many categories (greater than 12). The labels are easier to read displayed in the proper orientation.

1. Go to the sheet tab bar and click on **New Worksheet**. Then Double-click the tab name to edit it; type **Revenue by Sales Manager** and hit **Enter** or click on the canvas.

2. Drag the **Revenue** field to the **Columns** shelf. Then, drag the **Sales Manager** field to the **Row** shelf.

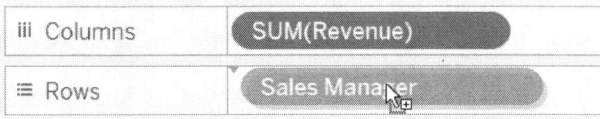

iii Columns	SUM(Revenue)
≡ Rows	Sales Manager

3. Go to Data pane and drag the **Region** and drop it on the **Color** area in the **Marks** as the image below.

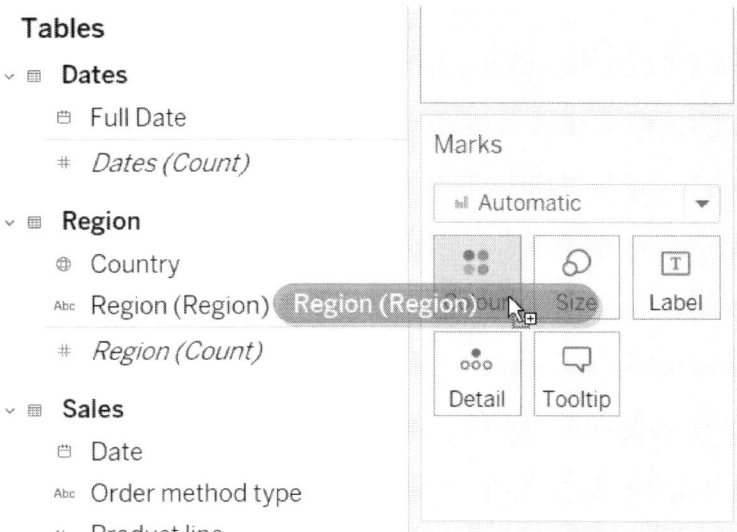

Tables

- ⊞ **Dates**
  - 🗓 Full Date
  - \# *Dates (Count)*
- ⊞ **Region**
  - ⊕ Country
  - Abc Region (Region)
  - \# *Region (Count)*
- ⊞ **Sales**
  - 🗓 Date
  - Abc Order method type
  - \# Product line

Marks

| ᵘ Automatic | ▼ |

⠿	🎨	T Label
Region (Region)	Size	
₀₀₀ Detail	💬 Tooltip	

4. Go to the Columns shelf and click on **Revenue** pill to select it.

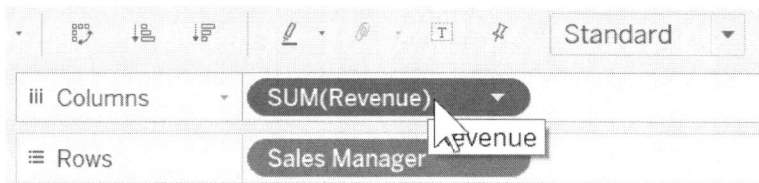

| ⠿ | ⬇ | ⬇ | ✏ ▼ | 📎 ▼ | T | ⚡ | Standard ▼ |

iii Columns	▼	SUM(Revenue) ▼
≡ Rows		Sales Manager

Revenue

5. Click on Sort Descending.

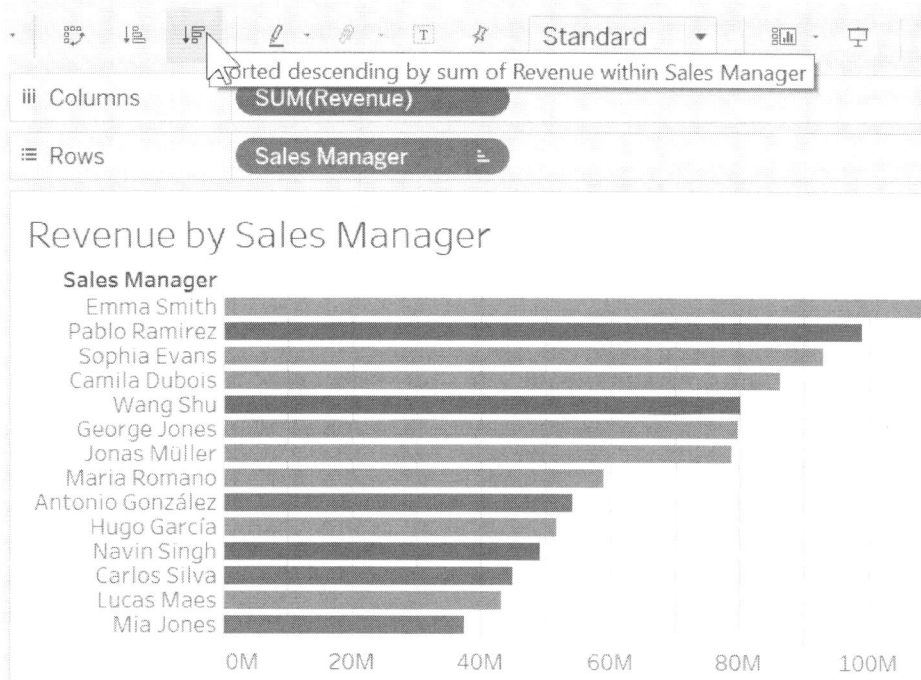

6. Go to **Marks**, click on **Color,** and change the **Opacity** to **85%**.

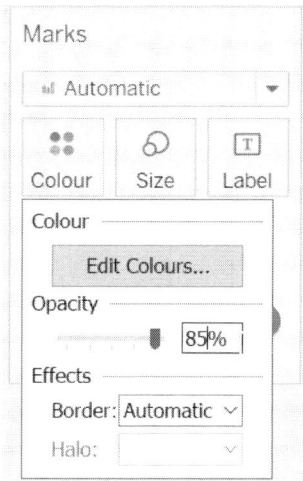

7. Go to the **Toolbar**, **Fit,** and select **Entire View**.

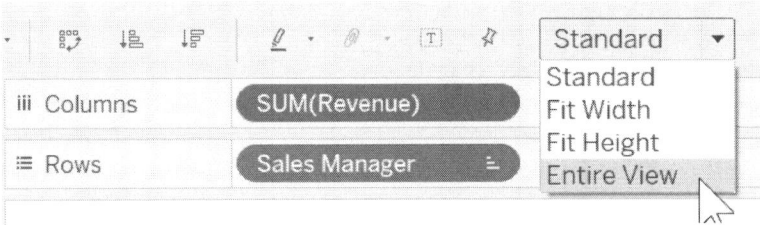

8. The Bar Chart should look like the image below.

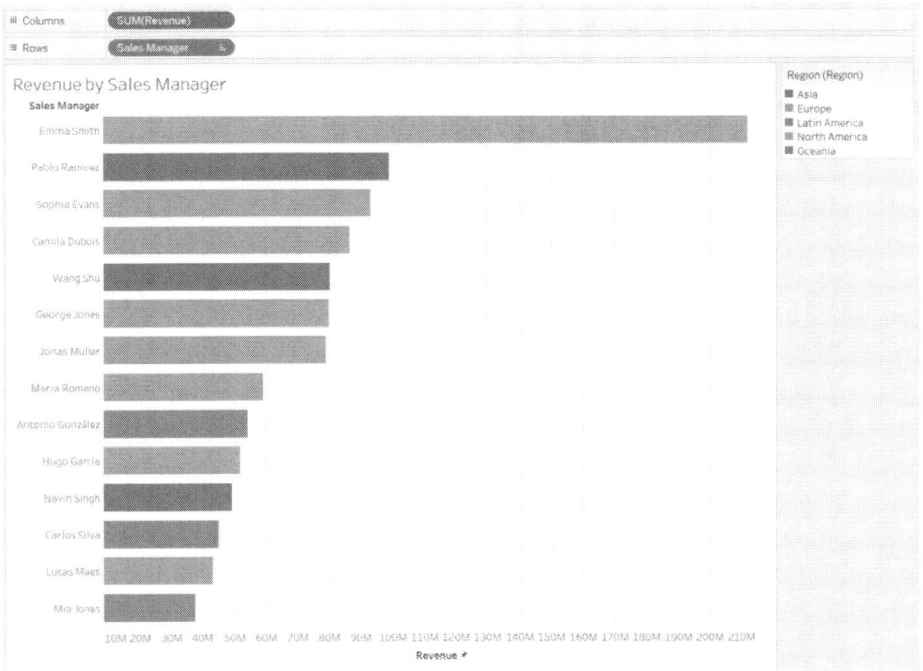

Chapter **5**

Creating Filters

14.   Filter by Region

1. Go to the sheet tab bar and click on **New Worksheet**. Then Double-click the tab name to edit it; type **Filter by Region** and hit **Enter** or click on the canvas.

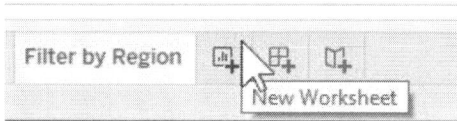

2. Drag the **Region** from the data pane and drop it on **Marks**.

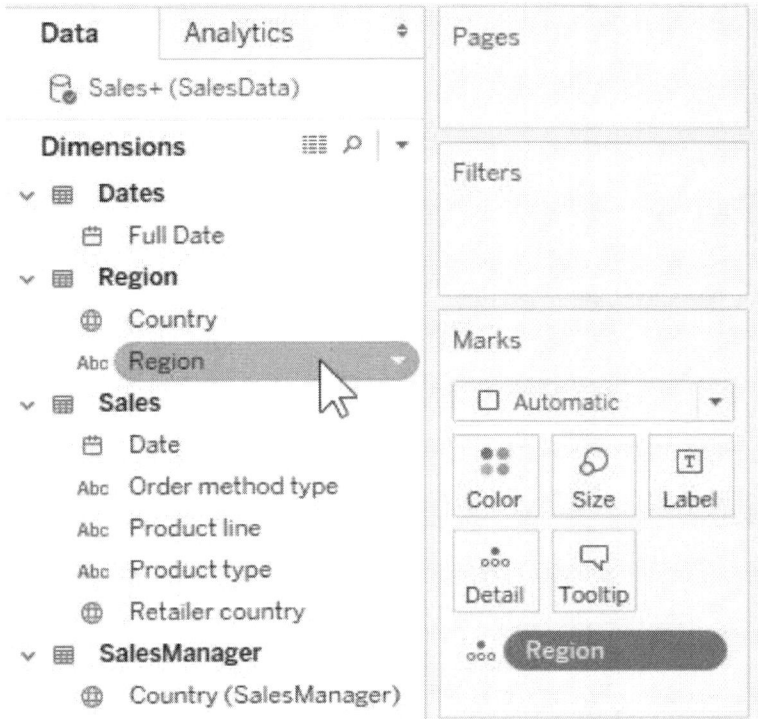

3. Change it to **Label**.

4. The region list should look like the image below.

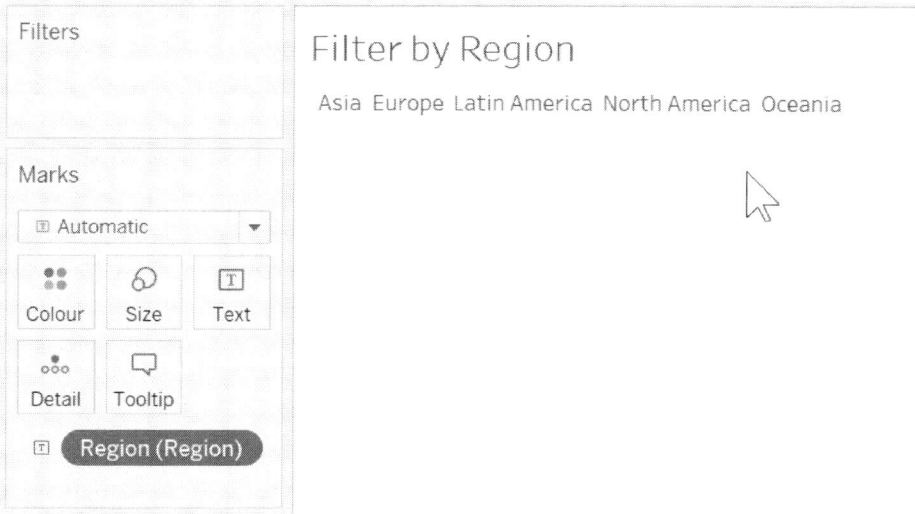

15. Filter by Year

1. Go to the sheet tab bar and click on **New Worksheet**. Double-click the tab name to edit it; type **Filter by Year** and hit **Enter** or click on the canvas.

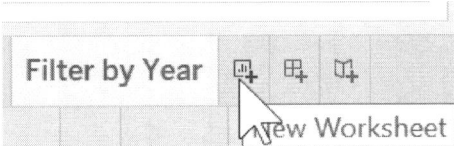

2. Go to **Sales** and drag the **Date** from the data pane and drop it on the **Text** area in the **Marks**. Then, click on **Size** and move the **Slider** to the second mark.

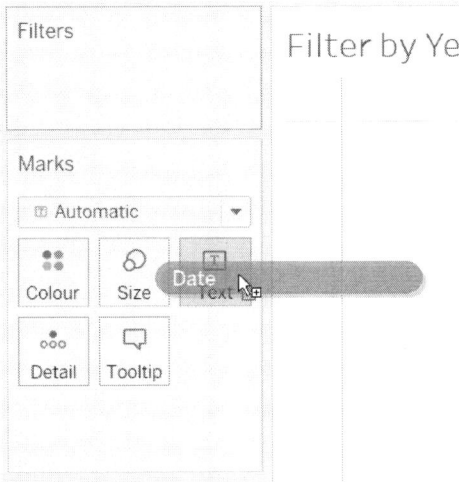

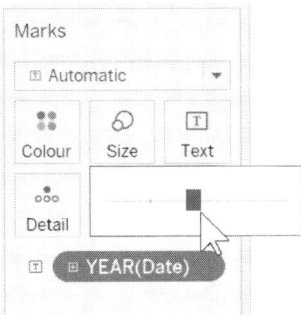

16. Filter by Product Line

1. Go to the sheet tab bar and click on **New Worksheet**. Double-click the tab name to edit it; type **Filter Product Line** and hit **Enter** or click on the canvas.

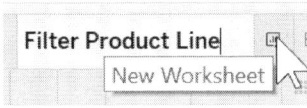

2. Go to **Sales**, drag the **Product line** field from the data pane and drop it on the **Text** area in the **Marks**.

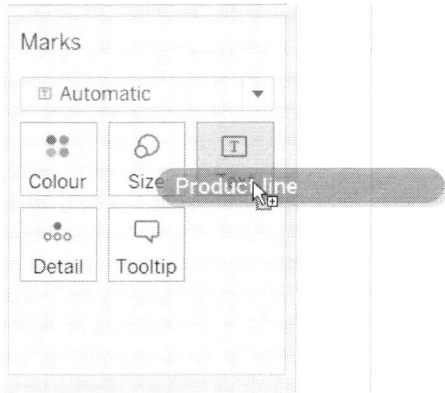

3. The Product Line list should look like the image below.

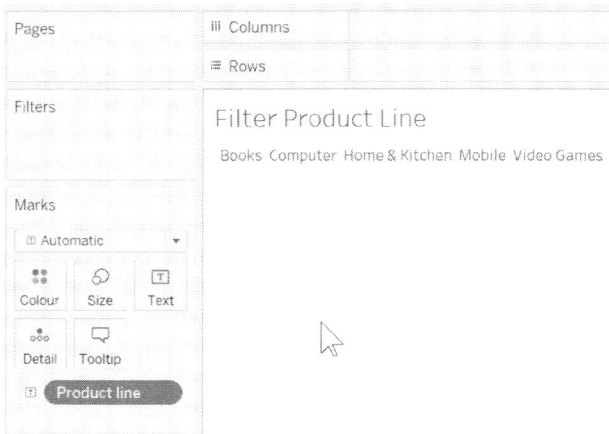

Chapter **6**

Building the Sales Dashboard

A dashboard is a graphical interface with a collection of views that allows you to compare various data simultaneously. For instance, if you have a set of views that you review on a daily basis, you can create a dashboard that groups all the views rather than navigate to separate reports.

17.   Creating a Dashboard

1. Go to the sheet tab bar and click on **New Dashboard**. Then Double-click the tab name to edit it; type **Sales Dashboard** and hit **Enter** or click on the canvas.

2. To move this tab, click on the **Sales Dashboard** tab, hold the mouse button to drag and drop it after the **Data Source**.

Data Source	Revenue	Total Cost	Gross Margir

3. Right-click the Sales Dashboard tab click on **Color,** and select the **Blue** color.

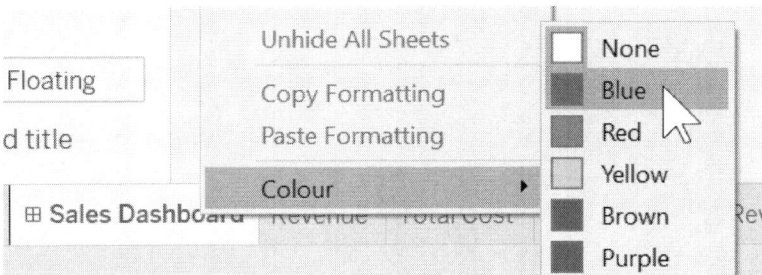

	Unhide All Sheets		None
Floating	Copy Formatting		Blue
d title	Paste Formatting		Red
	Colour ▶		Yellow
⊞ Sales Dashboard			Brown
			Purple

4. The Dashboard sidebar on the left gives you the option to change the Dashboard Layout and add the visuals you have created (Sheets) and Objects.

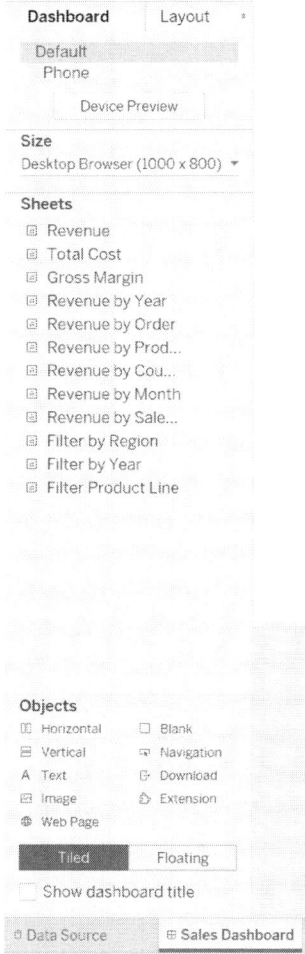

Dashboard	Layout
Default	
Phone	

Device Preview

Size

Desktop Browser (1000 x 800) ▾

Sheets

⊞ Revenue
⊞ Total Cost
⊞ Gross Margin
⊞ Revenue by Year
⊞ Revenue by Order
⊞ Revenue by Prod...
⊞ Revenue by Cou...
⊞ Revenue by Month
⊞ Revenue by Sale...
⊞ Filter by Region
⊞ Filter by Year
⊞ Filter Product Line

Objects

⊞ Horizontal	☐ Blank
⊟ Vertical	☞ Navigation
A Text	⬇ Download
⊞ Image	⬠ Extension
⊕ Web Page	

Tiled	Floating

☐ Show dashboard title

⬭ Data Source	⊞ Sales Dashboard

5. Go to the **Dashboard** tab, **Size**, and select **Fixed size**. Then, select the option **PowerPoint** (1600x900).

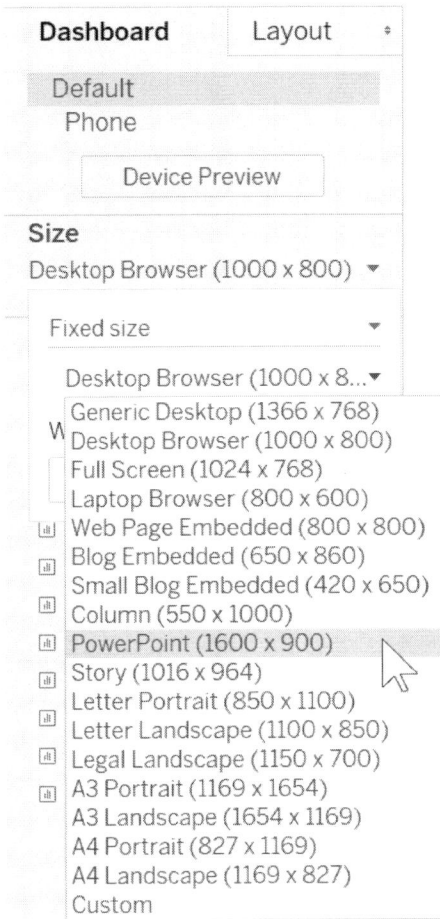

Dashboard	Layout	⇕

Default
   Phone

     Device Preview

Size
Desktop Browser (1000 x 800) ▼

  Fixed size   ▼

  Desktop Browser (1000 x 8...▼

Generic Desktop (1366 x 768)
Desktop Browser (1000 x 800)
Full Screen (1024 x 768)
Laptop Browser (800 x 600)
Web Page Embedded (800 x 800)
Blog Embedded (650 x 860)
Small Blog Embedded (420 x 650)
Column (550 x 1000)
PowerPoint (1600 x 900)
Story (1016 x 964)
Letter Portrait (850 x 1100)
Letter Landscape (1100 x 850)
Legal Landscape (1150 x 700)
A3 Portrait (1169 x 1654)
A3 Landscape (1654 x 1169)
A4 Portrait (827 x 1169)
A4 Landscape (1169 x 827)
Custom

6. Click on **Format** tab and select **Dashboard**.

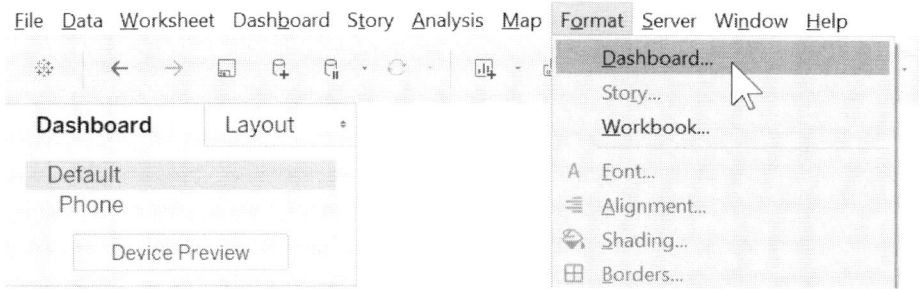

7. Go to the **Side Bar**, **Format Dashboard**, **Dashboard Shading**, and change it to a light gray.

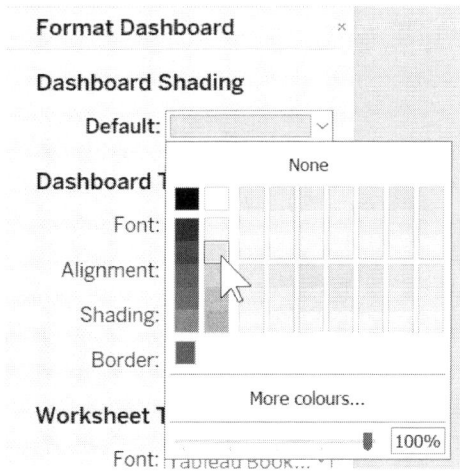

8. Close the Format Dashboard.

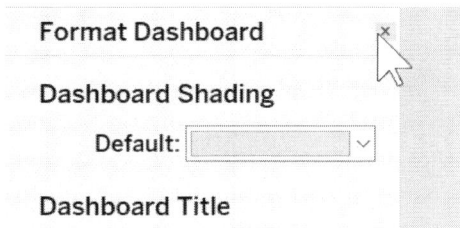

18.   Adding an Image

1. Go to the Side Bar, **Objects**, and click on **Floating**. This will give to visuals and objects in the Dashboard the ability to be placed anywhere.

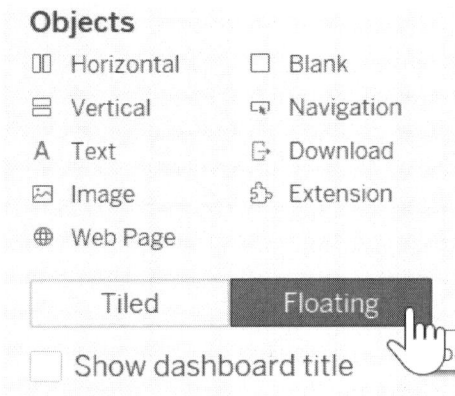

Objects

▯▯	Horizontal	☐	Blank
▤	Vertical	⌑	Navigation
A	Text	⊟	Download
▨	Image	⅋	Extension
⊕	Web Page		

Tiled	Floating

☐ Show dashboard title

2. Go to **Objects** and click on **Image**

Objects

▯▯	Horizontal	☐	Blank
▤	Vertical	⌑	Navigation
A	Text	⊟	Download
▨	Image	⅋	Extension
⊕	Web Page		

Tiled	Floating

☐ Show dashboard title

3. Double-click or drag the **Image Button** to the canvas.

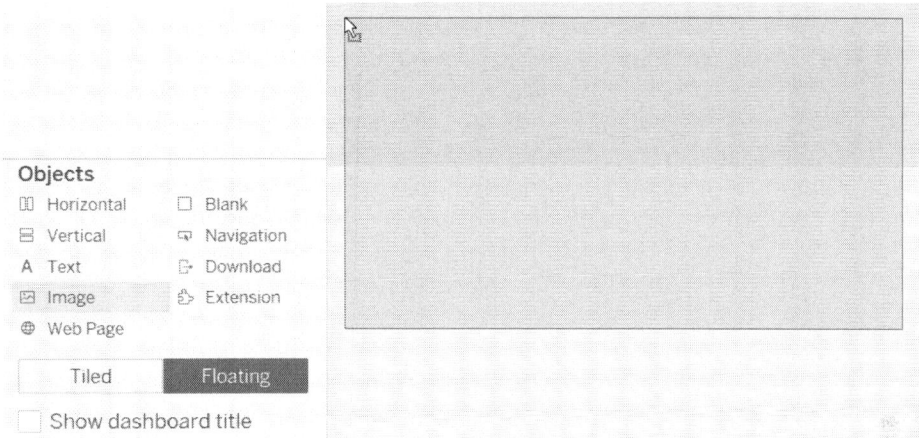

Objects

🎮 Horizontal	☐ Blank
⊟ Vertical	🖘 Navigation
A Text	🕞 Download
🖾 Image	🕭 Extension
⊕ Web Page	

Tiled	Floating

☐ Show dashboard title

4. The **Edit Image Object** window will appear. Go to **Image** and click on **Choose**.

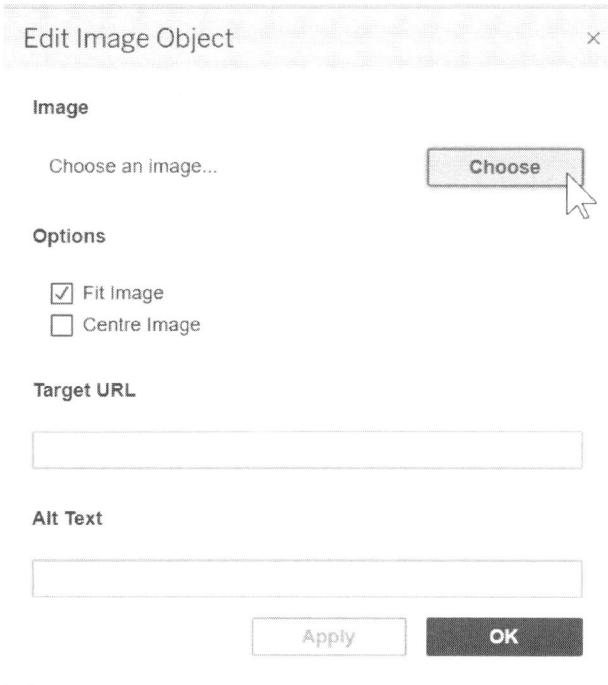

Edit Image Object   ×

Image

Choose an image...   [Choose]

Options

☑ Fit Image
☐ Centre Image

Target URL

[   ]

Alt Text

[   ]

[Apply]   [OK]

5. Select the **Create and Learn** image you have downloaded from https://www.createandlearn.net/bifiles

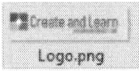

6. Check the options **Fit Image** and **Center Image**. Then include the **Target URL** createandlearn.net. Click **OK**.

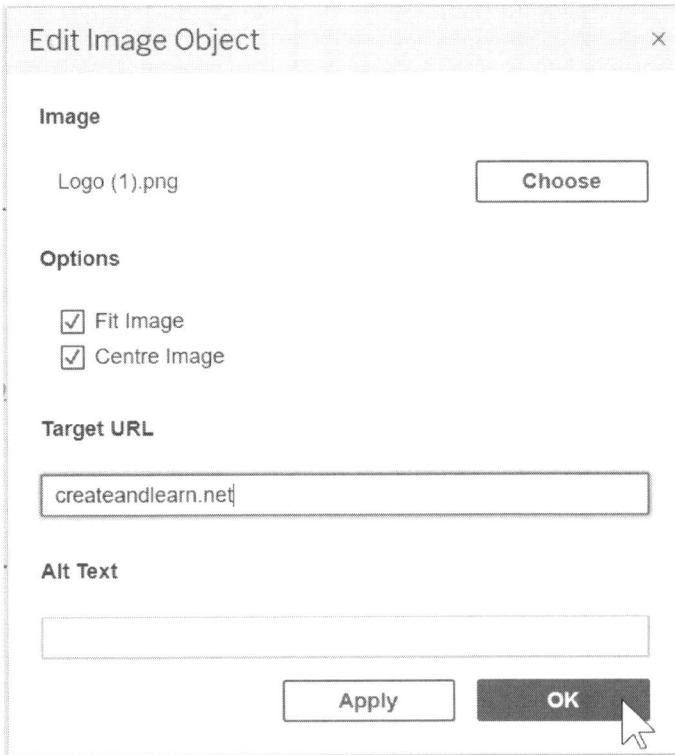

7. Use the handle at the top to move the image.

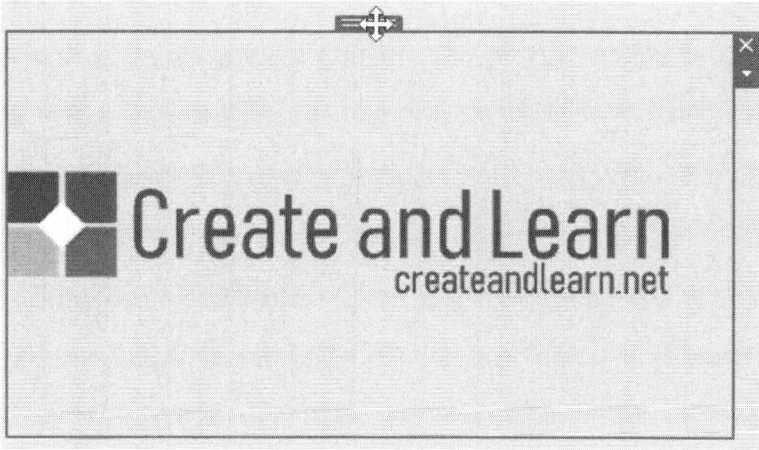

8. Select the image and go to the **Layout** tab.

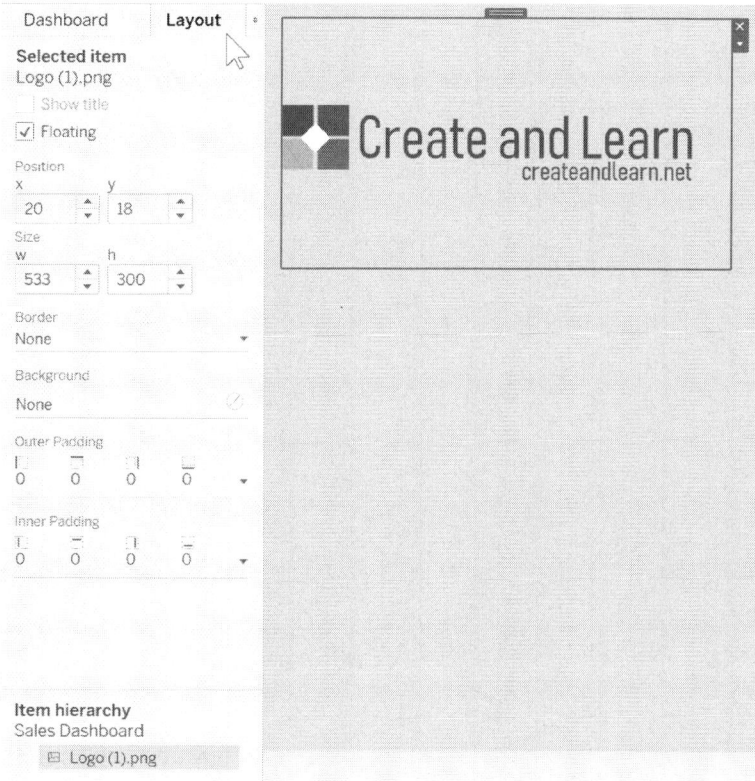

9. Click on **Background** and change the color to white.

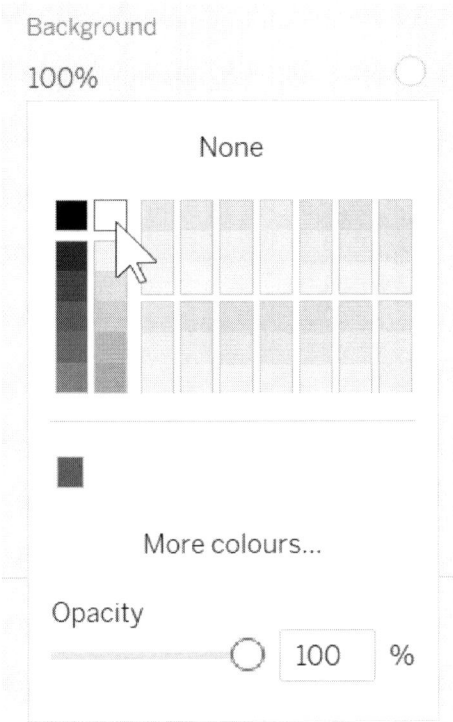

Background

100%

None

More colours...

Opacity

100 %

10. Go to **Position** and set the **X** to 10, **Y** to 10. Then change the size **w** to 370 and **h** to 122.

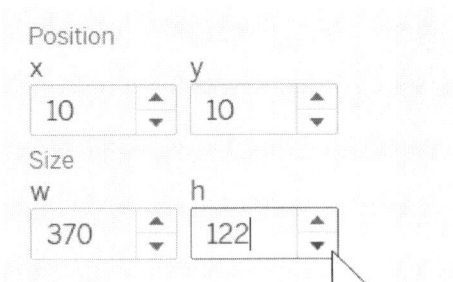

Position

x

10

y

10

Size

w

370

h

122

11. The Dashboard should look like the image below.

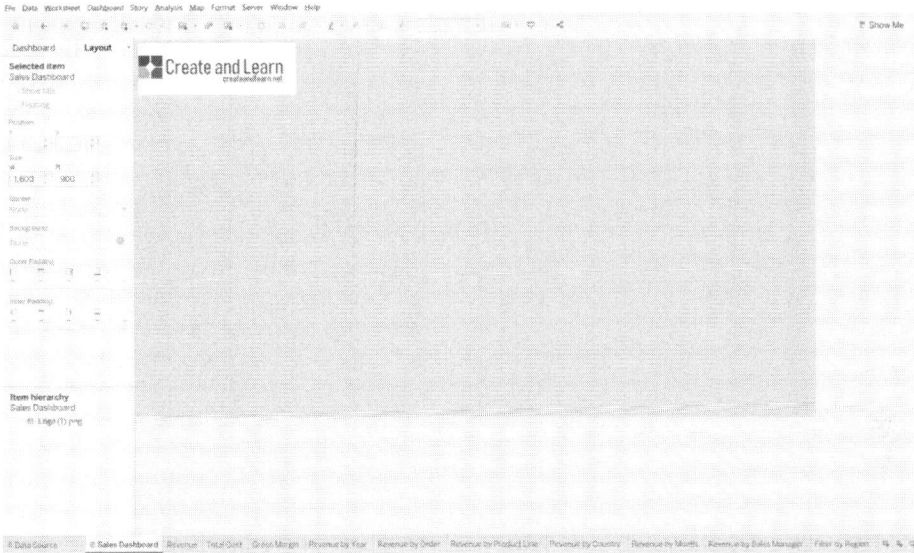

19.　Adding the Bar Chart - Revenue by Year

1. Go to the Side Bar, Objects, and select Floating.

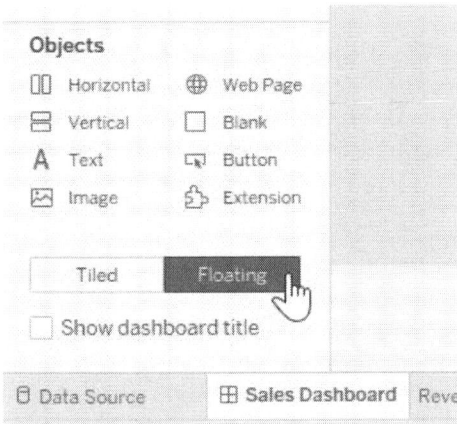

2. Go to the **Sheets** area and double-click or drag the **Revenue by Year** to add in the Dashboard.

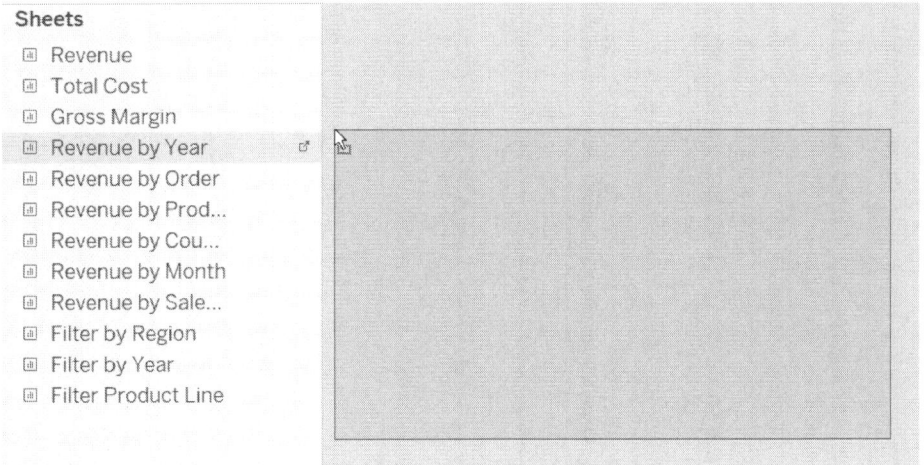

3. With the chart selected, go to the **Layout** tab.

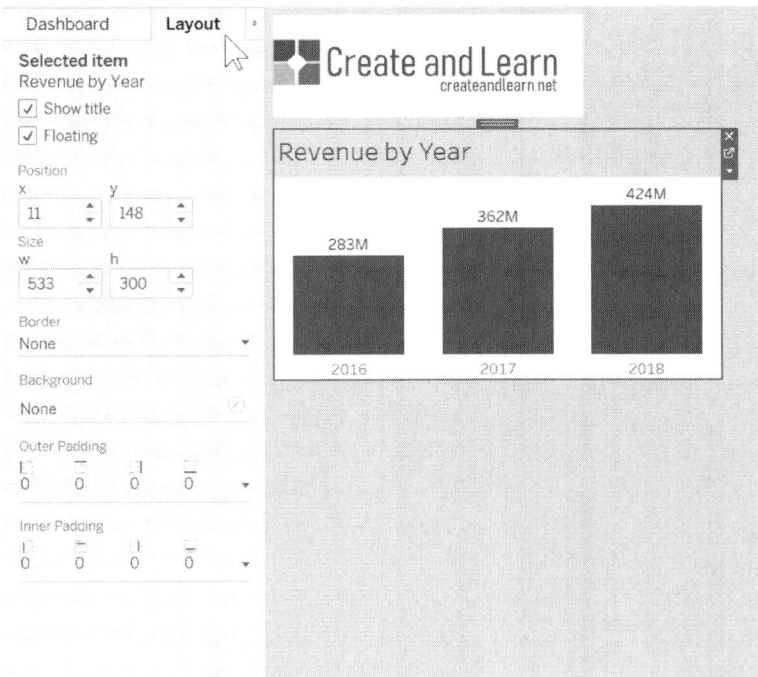

4. Go to **Position** and set the **X** to 10, **Y** to 145. Then change the **Size** **w** to 370 and **h** to 375.

☑ Floating

Position
X
10

y
145

Size
w
370

h
375

Border
None

Background
None

Outer Padding

Revenue by Year

283M

362M

424M

2016   2017   2018

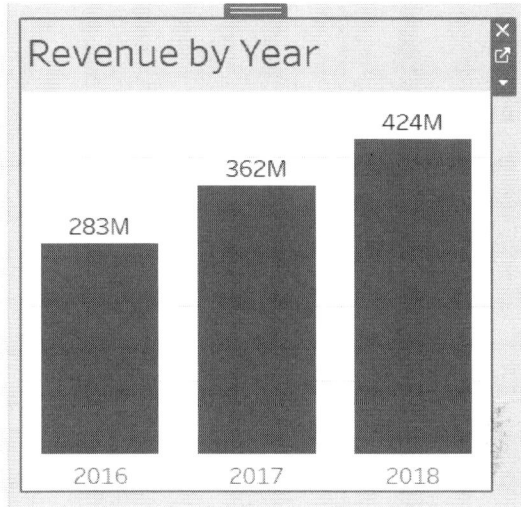

5. Click on **Background** and change the color to white.

Background
100%

None

More colours...

Opacity
100   %

6. Right-click the chart title and click on **Format Title.**

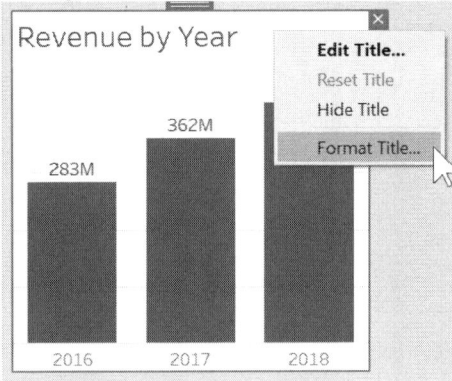

7. Go to the sidebar, **Format Title and Caption**, **Title**, **Shading** and select the white color.

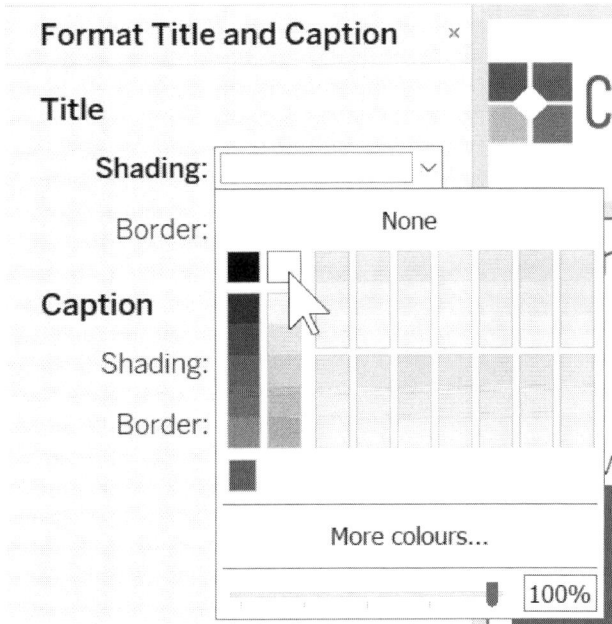

Format Title and Caption ×

Title

Shading:

Border:

Caption

Shading:

Border:

None

More colours...

100%

8. Close the sidebar.

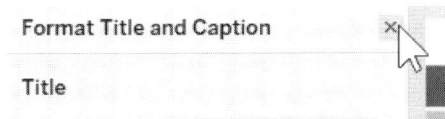

Format Title and Caption ×

Title

20. Adding the Pie Chart - Revenue by Order Method

1. Go to the **Side Bar**, **Objects,** and select **Floating**. Then, go to the **Sheets** area and double-click or drag the **Revenue by Order** to add in the Dashboard.

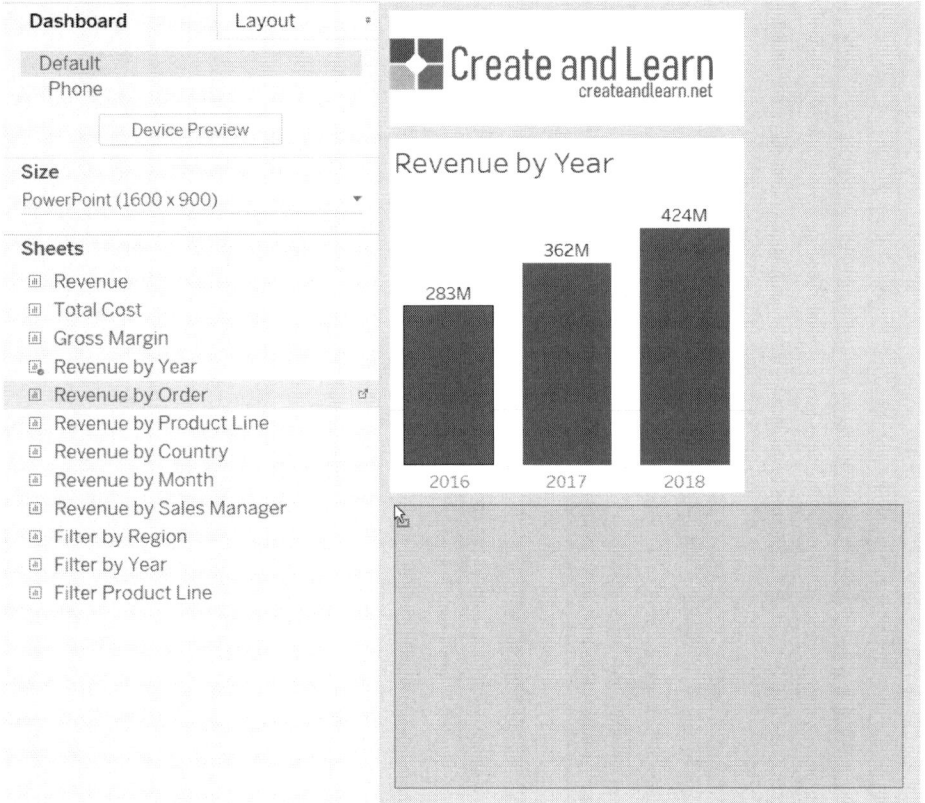

2. Go to **Layout** tab, **Position,** and set the **X** to 10, **Y** to 535. Then change the size **w** to 370 and **h** to 301.

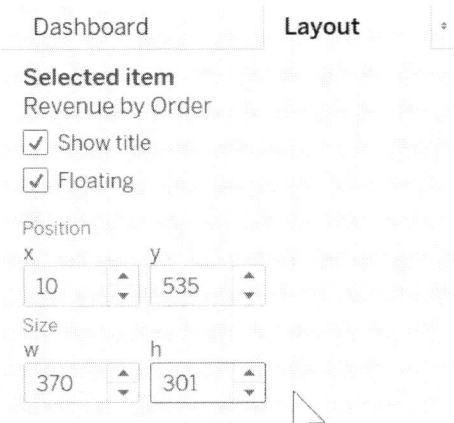

Dashboard	Layout	⋮
Selected item		
Revenue by Order		
☑ Show title		
☑ Floating		
Position		
x	y	
10	535	
Size		
w	h	
370	301	

3. Select the **Revenue** legend from the Pie Chart and click on **Remove from Dashboard**.

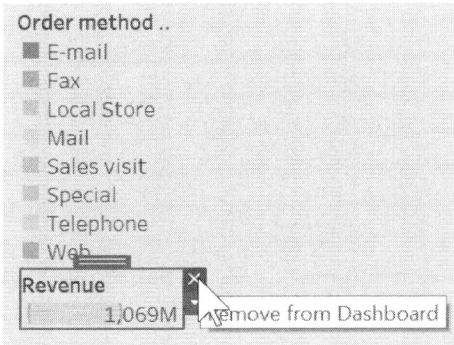

Order method ..
- E-mail
- Fax
- Local Store
- Mail
- Sales visit
- Special
- Telephone
- Web

Revenue
1,069M ✕ Remove from Dashboard

4. Select the **Order method type** legend, click on the down-arrow, **Arrange items**, and select **Multiple columns**.

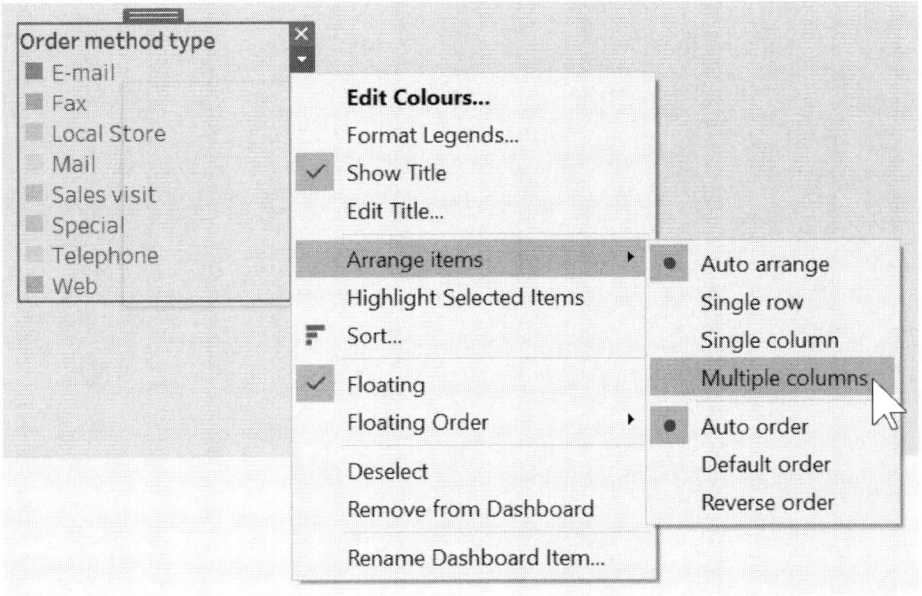

Order method type		
☐ E-mail	**Edit Colours...**	
☐ Fax	Format Legends...	
☐ Local Store	✓ Show Title	
☐ Mail	Edit Title...	
☐ Sales visit		
☐ Special	Arrange items ▶	● Auto arrange
☐ Telephone	Highlight Selected Items	Single row
☐ Web	☰ Sort...	Single column
		Multiple columns
	✓ Floating	● Auto order
	Floating Order ▶	Default order
	Deselect	Reverse order
	Remove from Dashboard	
	Rename Dashboard Item...	

5. Use the handle to move the legend to the bottom of the chart.

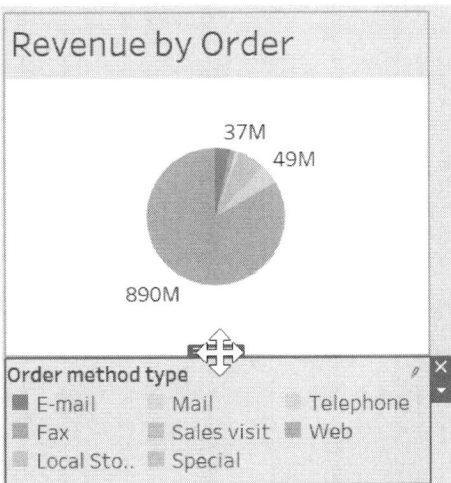

Revenue by Order

37M
49M
890M

Order method type		
☐ E-mail	☐ Mail	☐ Telephone
☐ Fax	☐ Sales visit	☐ Web
☐ Local Sto..	☐ Special	

6. With the legend selected, go to **Layout** tab, **Position** and set the **X** to 10, **Y** to 836. Then change the size **w** to 370 and **h** to 60. Click on **Background** and change the color to white.

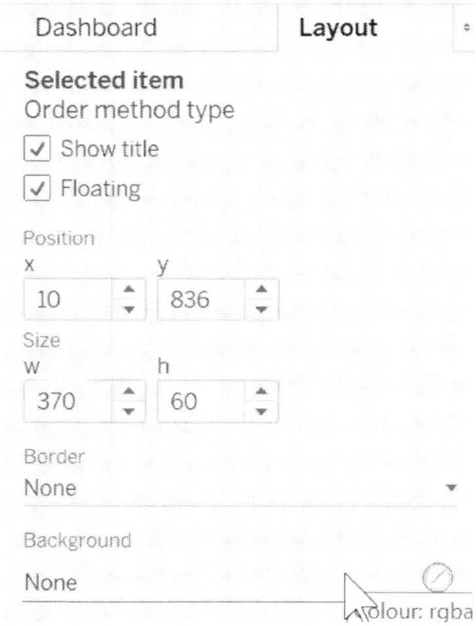

Dashboard	Layout

Selected item
Order method type

☑ Show title

☑ Floating

Position

x

| 10 | | y | 836 | |

Size

w

| 370 | | h | 60 | |

Border

None

Background

None

Colour: rgba

7. Click on the down-arrow again and uncheck the **Show Title** option.

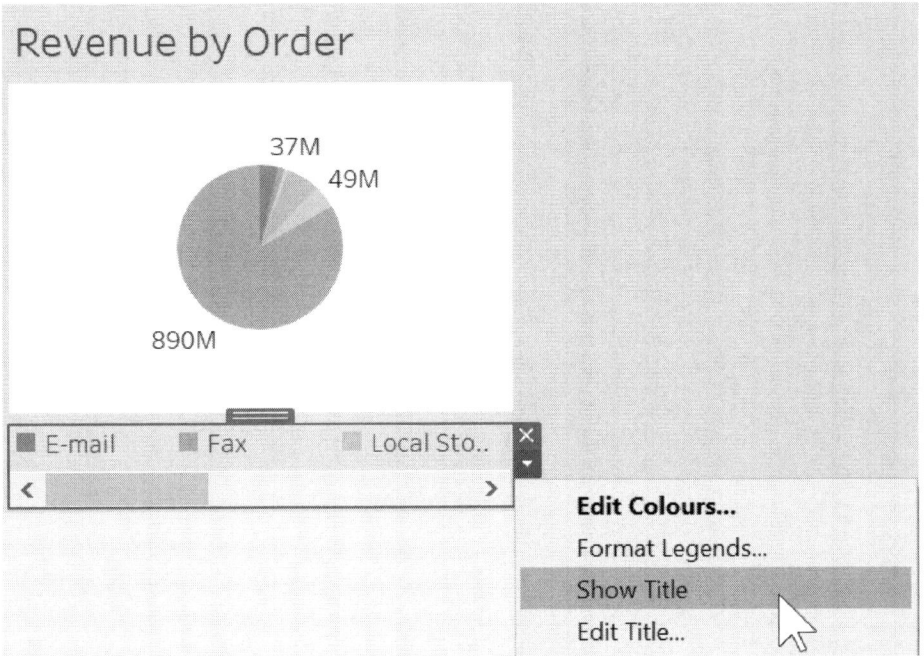

8. Go to **Layout** tab, **Position,** and set the **X** to 10, **Y** to 825. Then change the size **w** to 370 and **h** to 60. Click on **Background** and change the color to white.

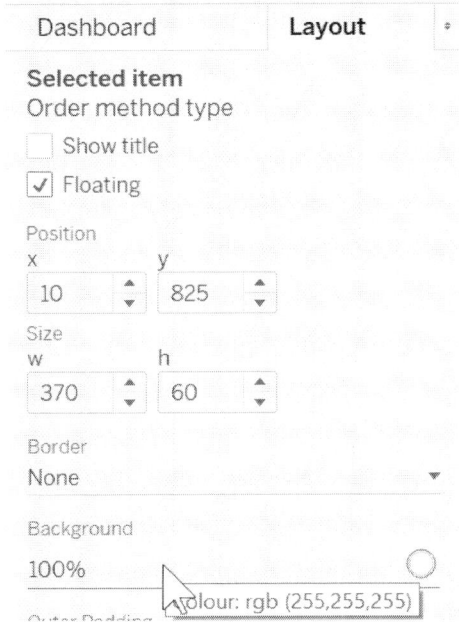

Dashboard	Layout	⚙

Selected item
Order method type

☐ Show title

☑ Floating

Position
x   y

| 10 | ⬍ | 825 | ⬍ |

Size
w   h

| 370 | ⬍ | 60 | ⬍ |

Border
None   ▼

Background

100%   ◯

Colour: rgb (255,255,255)

9. Right-click the chart title and click on **Format Title**

Edit Title...

Reset Title

Hide Title

Format Title...

10. Go to the sidebar, **Format Title, and Caption**, **Title**, **Shading** and select the white color.

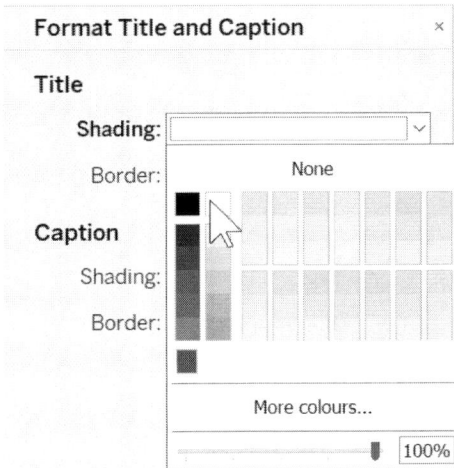

11. Close the Format Title and Caption in the Side Bar.

12. To increase the pie chart's size, click on **Revenue by Order** tab.

13. Go to **Marks** card, **Size**, and increase the size as the image below.

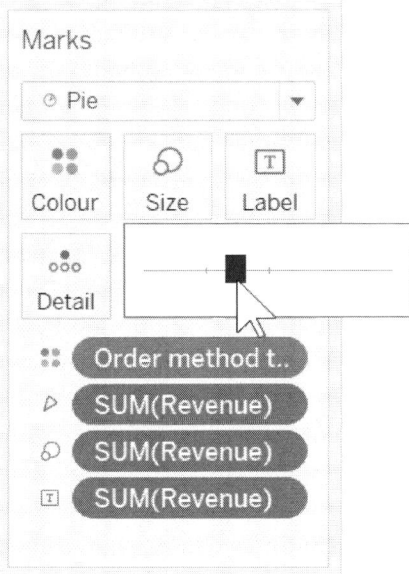

14. The Dashboard should look like the image below.

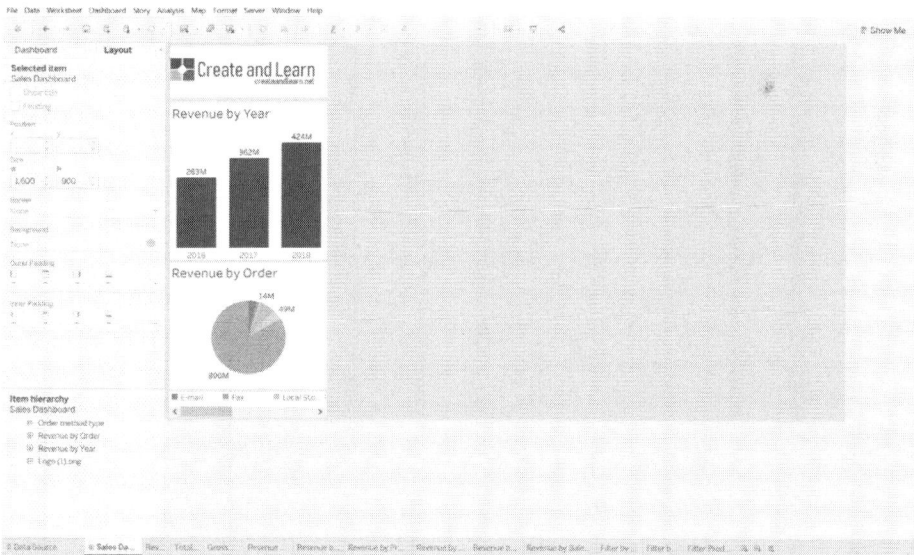

21. Add the Line Chart - Revenue by Month

1. Go to the **Side Bar**, **Objects,** and select **Floating**. Then, go to the **Sheets** area and double-click or drag the **Revenue by Month** to add in the Dashboard.

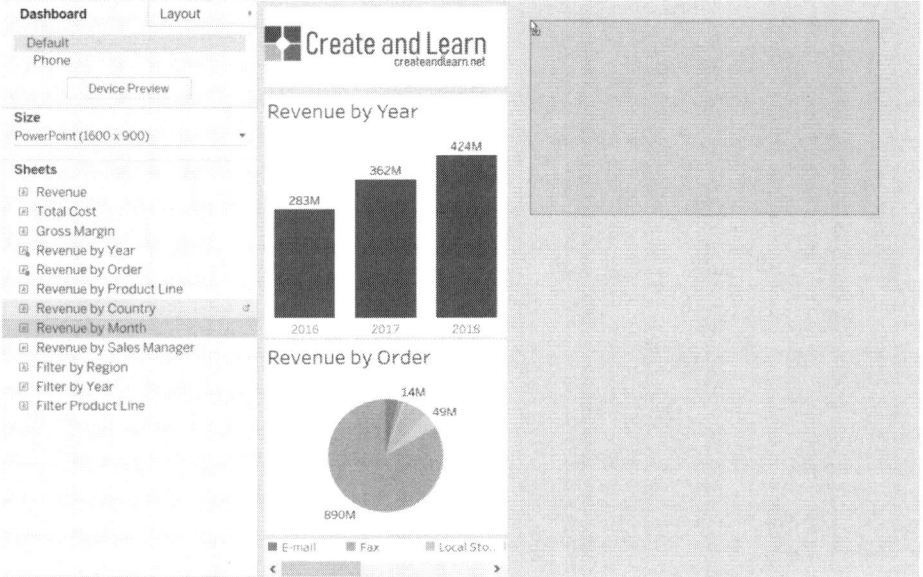

2. Go to **Layout** tab, **Position,** and set the **X** to 395, **Y** to 145. Then change the size **w** to 685 and **h** to 375. Click on **Background** and change the color to white.

| Dashboard | Layout | ⊕ |

Selected item
Region (Region)

☑ Show title

☑ Floating

Position
x   y

| 983 | ▲▼ | 44 | ▲▼ |

Size
w   h

| 155 | ▲▼ | 151 | ▲▼ |

Border

None ▼

Background

100%   ◯

Colour: rgb (255,255,255)
None

▼

▼

3. Select the **Region** legend, click on the down-arrow, **Arrange items**, and select **Single row**.

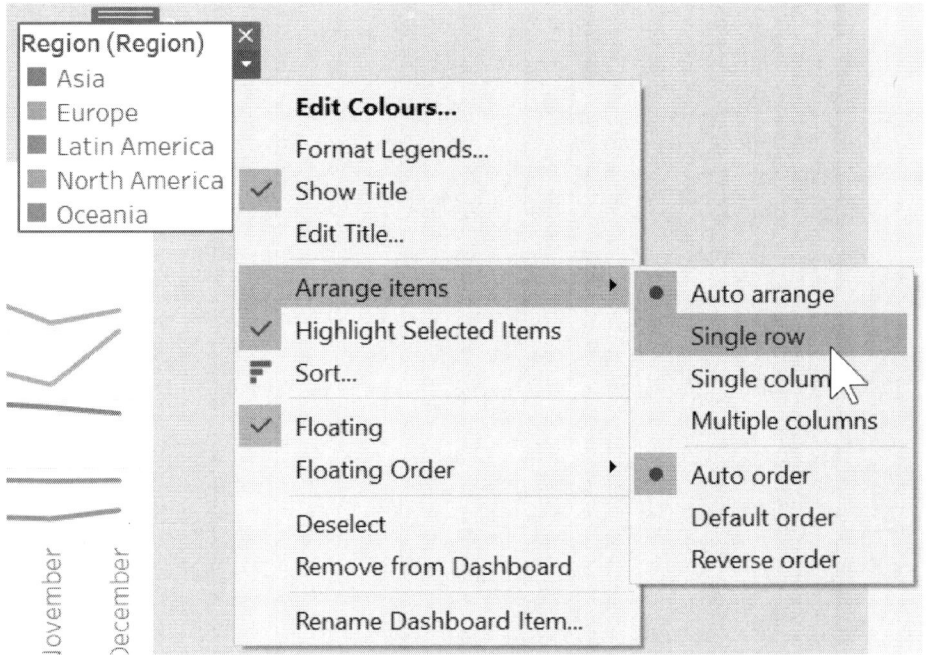

4. Click on the down-arrow again and uncheck the **Show Title** option.

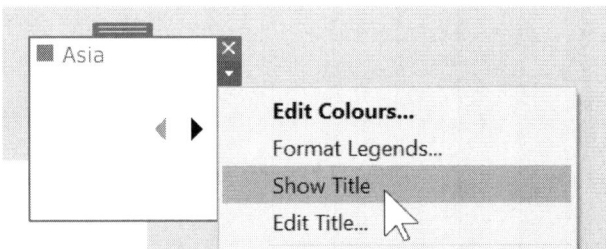

5. Resize the legend to fit close to the chart title.

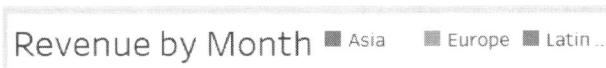

6. Reduce the size of the spaces between the legend items.

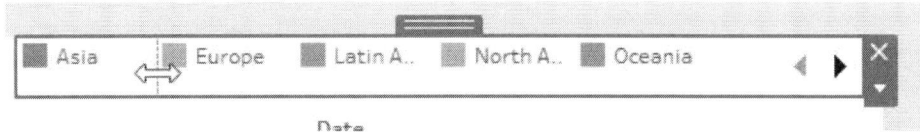

7. Click on the down-arrow and **Format Legends**.

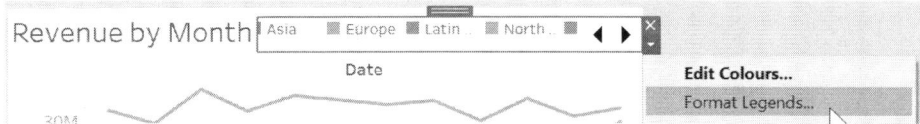

8. Go to the sidebar, **Format Legends**, **Body**, **Font,** and change the font size to **8**.

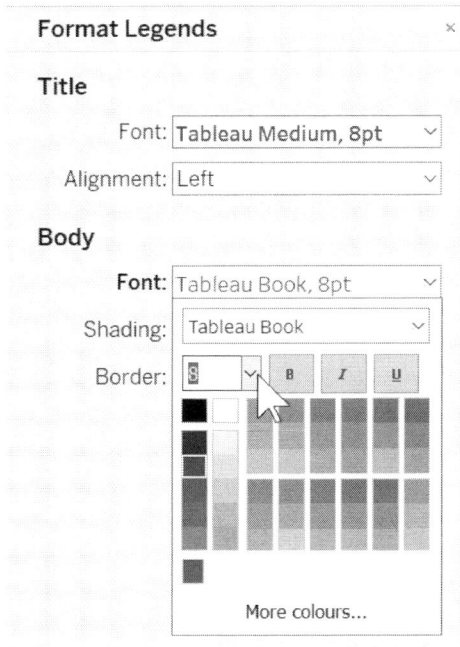

9. Right-click the chart title and click on **Format Title**

10. Go to the sidebar, **Format Title, and Caption**, **Title**, **Shading**, and select the white color.

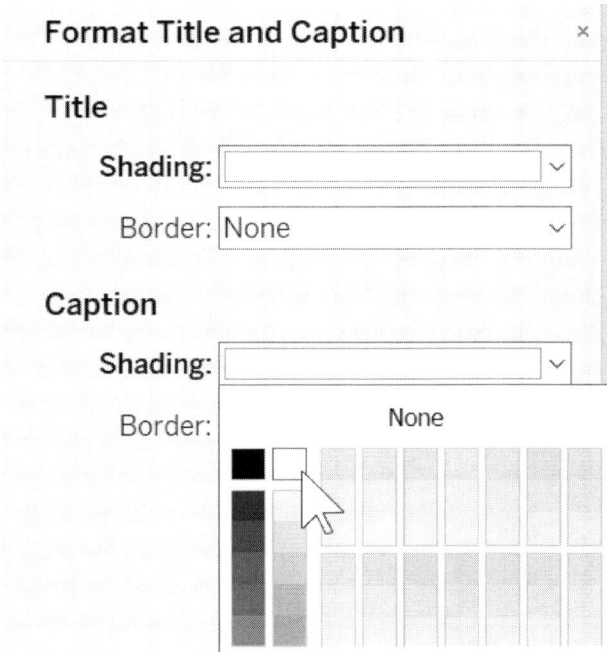

11. The Dashboard should look like the image below.

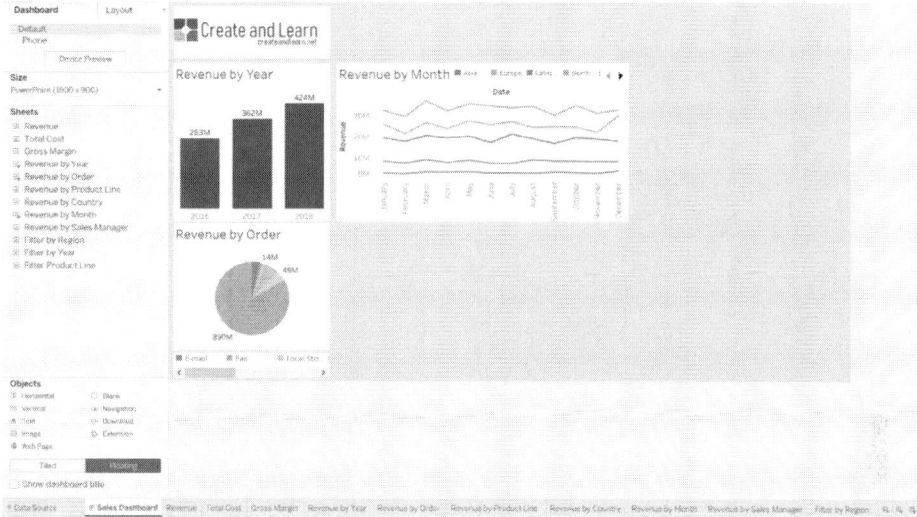

22. Add the Treemap - Revenue by Product Line

1. Go to the **Side Bar**, **Objects,** and select **Floating**. Then, go to the **Sheets** area and double-click or drag the **Revenue by Product Line** to add in the Dashboard.

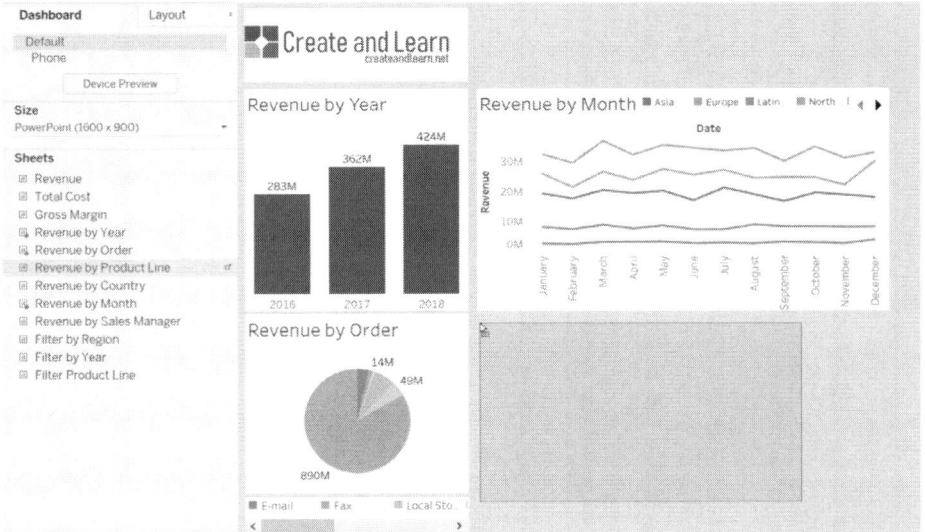

2. Go to **Layout** tab, **Position,** and set the **X** to 395, **Y** to 535. Then change the size **w** to 685 and **h** to 350. Click on **Background** and change the color to white.

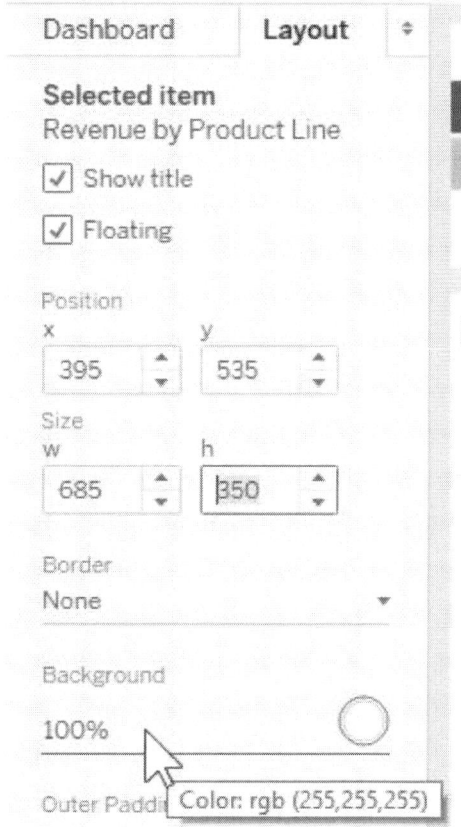

Dashboard	Layout	⇕

Selected item
Revenue by Product Line

☑ Show title

☑ Floating

Position
x   y
[395]⇅   [535]⇅

Size
w   h
[685]⇅   [350]⇅

Border
None   ▼

Background
100%   ◯

Outer Paddi | Color: rgb (255,255,255)

3. Select the **Product line** legend and click on **Remove from Dashboard**.

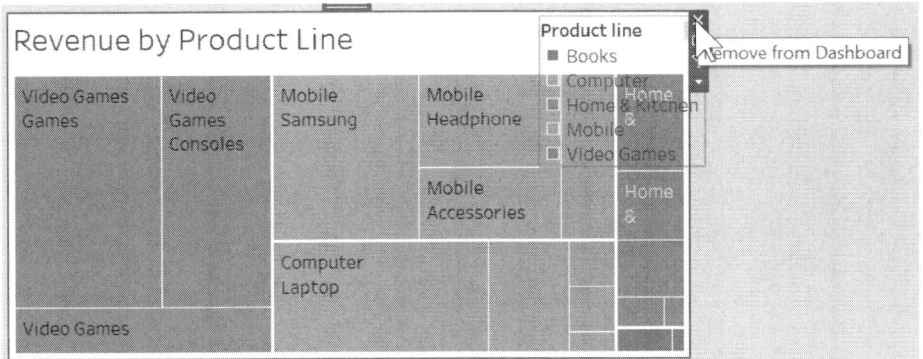

4. Right-click the chart title and click on **Format Title**

5. Go to the sidebar, **Format Title, and Caption**, **Title**, **Shading** and select the white color.

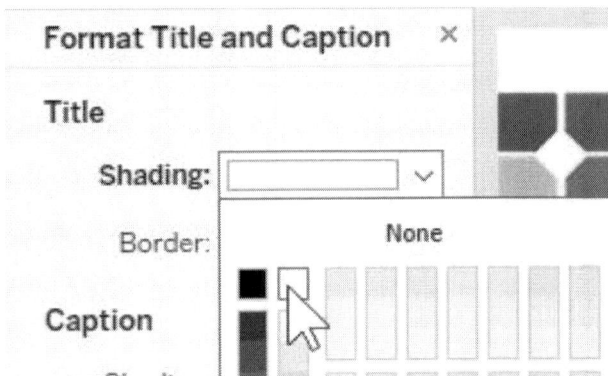

6. The Dashboard should look like the image below.

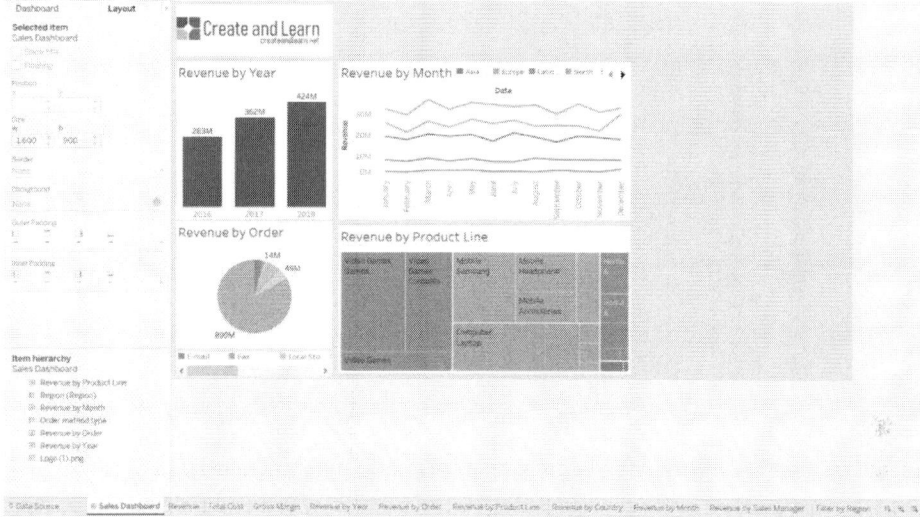

23. Add the Map - Revenue by Country

1. Go to the **Side Bar**, **Objects,** and select **Floating**. Then, go to the **Sheets** area and double-click or drag the **Revenue by Country** to add in the Dashboard.

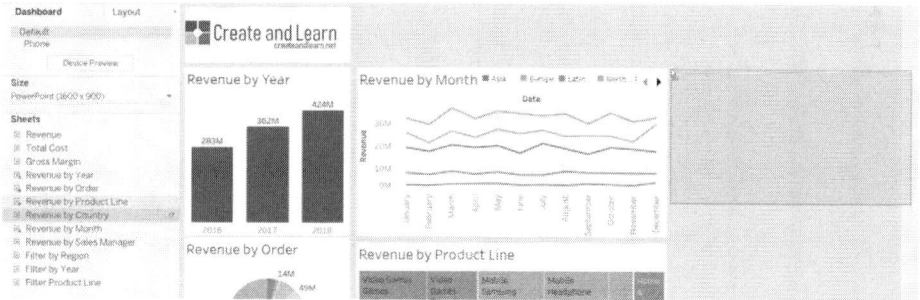

2. Go to **Layout** tab, **Position,** and set the **X** to 1094, **Y** to 145. Then change the size **w** to 500 and **h** to 375. Click on **Background** and change the color to white.

Dashboard	**Layout**	⬦

Selected item
Revenue by Country

☑ Show title

☑ Floating

Position

x   y

1,094 ⬍	144 ⬍

Size

w   h

500 ⬍	375 ⬍

Border

None   ▼

Background

100%

Colour:

3. Select the **Revenue** legend from the **Map** and click on **Remove from Dashboard**.

Revenue by Country

Revenue
- 37,505,254
- 100,000,000
- 150,000,000
- 211,930,232

4. Right-click the chart title and click on **Format Title**

Edit Title...

Reset Title

Hide Title

Format Title...

5. Go to the sidebar, **Format Title, and Caption**, **Title**, **Shading,** and select the white color.

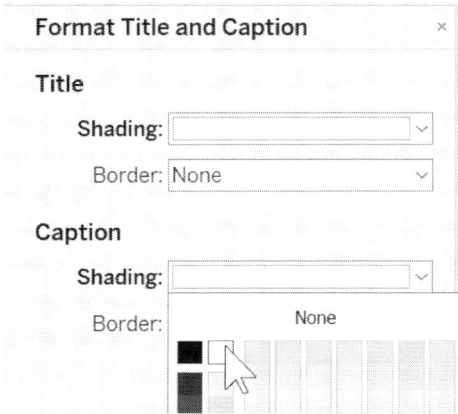

Format Title and Caption ✕

Title

Shading: [   ] ⌄

Border: [None   ] ⌄

Caption

Shading: [   ] ⌄

Border: None

6. The Dashboard should look like the image below.

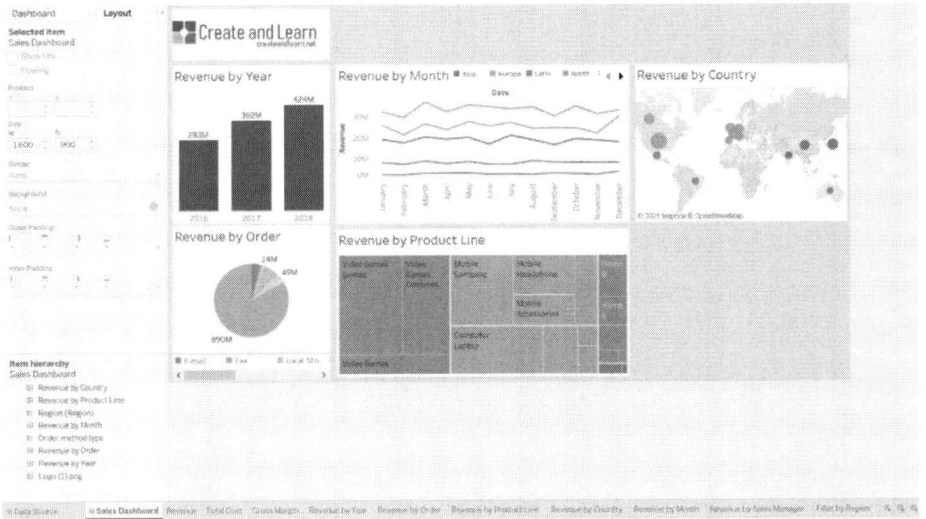

24. Bar Chart - Revenue by Year

1. Go to the Side Bar, Objects, and select **Floating**. Then, go to the **Sheets** area and double-click or drag the **Revenue by Sales Manager** to add in the Dashboard.

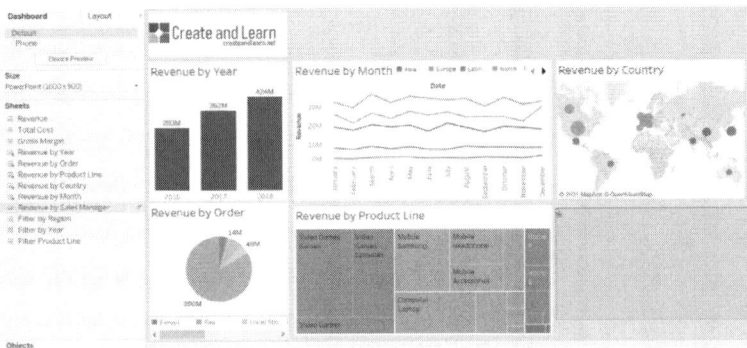

2. Go to **Layout** tab, **Position** and set the **X** to 1094, **Y** to 535. Then change the size **w** to 500 and **h** to 350. Click on **Background** and change the color to white.

Dashboard	Layout	⋮

Selected item
Revenue by Sales Manager

☑ Show title
☑ Floating

Position
x   y

| 1,094 ⏶⏷ | 535 ⏶⏷ |

Size
w   h

| 500 ⏶⏷ | 350 ⏶⏷ |

Border
None   ▼

Background
100%   ◯

None

3. Select the **chart**, click on the down-arrow, **Legends,** and click on
Color Legend (Region**).**

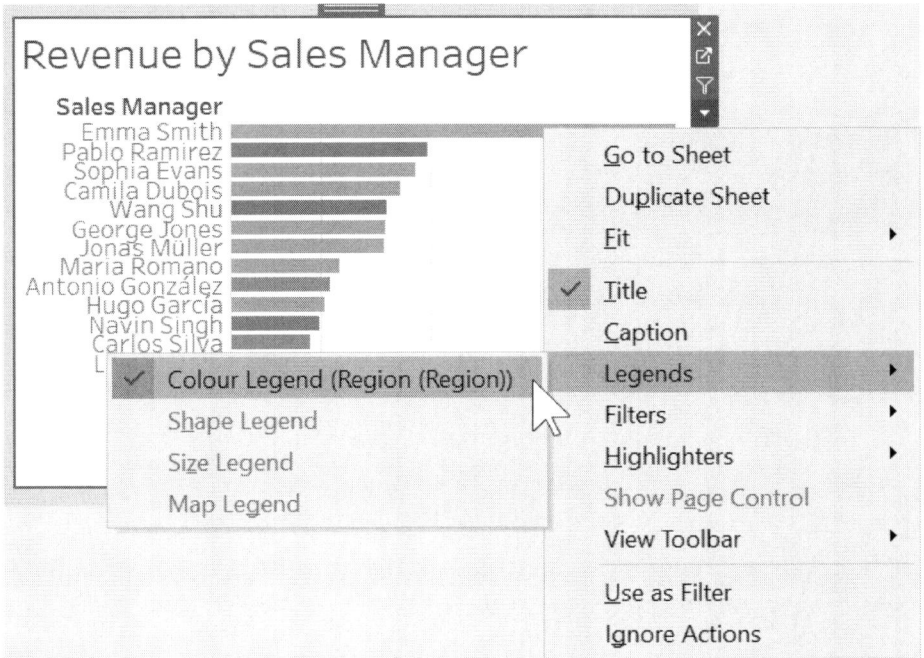

4. Select the **Region** legend, click on the down-arrow, **Arrange items**, and select **Single row.**

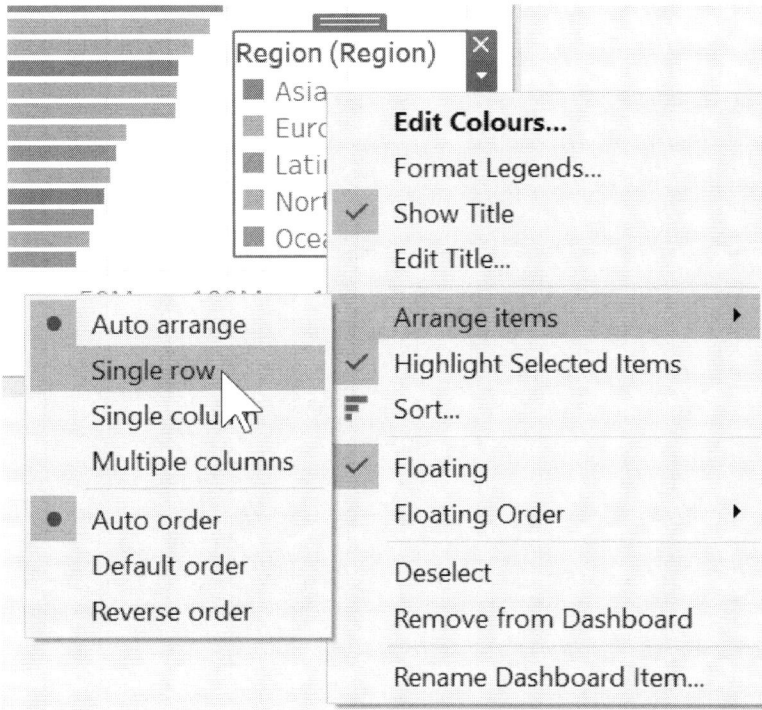

5. Click on the down-arrow again and uncheck the **Show Title** option.

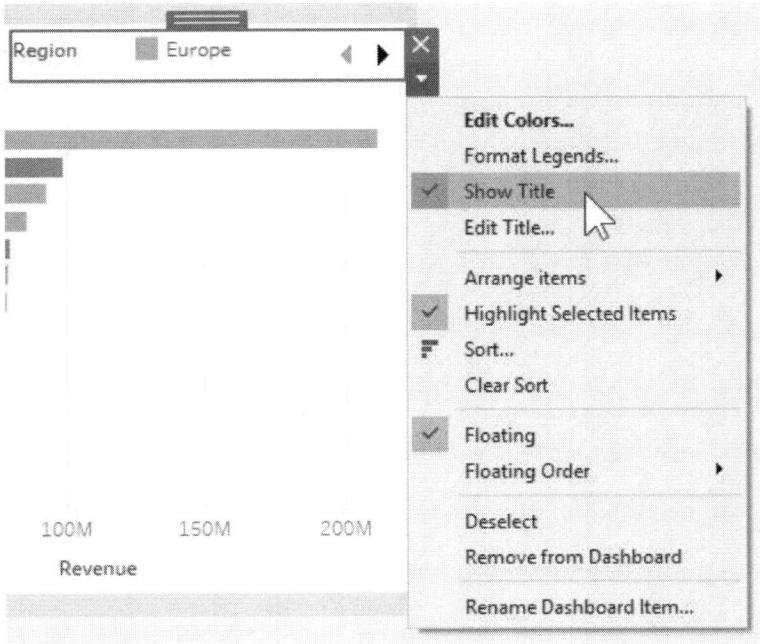

6. Right-click the **horizontal axis** and click on **Edit Axis**.

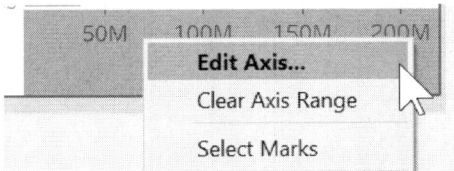

7. In the Edit Axis [Revenue] window, go to Axis Titles, and Title.

Edit Axis [Revenue]   ×

General   Tick Marks

Range

- ● Automatic   ☑ Include zero
- ○ Uniform axis range for all rows or columns
- ○ Independent axis ranges for each row or column
- ○ Fixed

| Automatic   ▼ | Automatic   ▼ |
| 0 | 222,526,743.504 |

Scale

- ☐ Reversed
- ☐ Logarithmic

  ● Positive   ○ Symmetric

Axis Titles

Title

Revenue

Subtitle

Subtitle   ☑ Automatic

↺ **Reset**

8. For the **Title** field type a single **space**. Note, that if you include a **space,** it will hide the title but keeping the axis.

Axis Titles

Title

> Title

Subtitle

Subtitle

☑ Automatic

9. Move the legend to the bottom and resize it as in the image below.

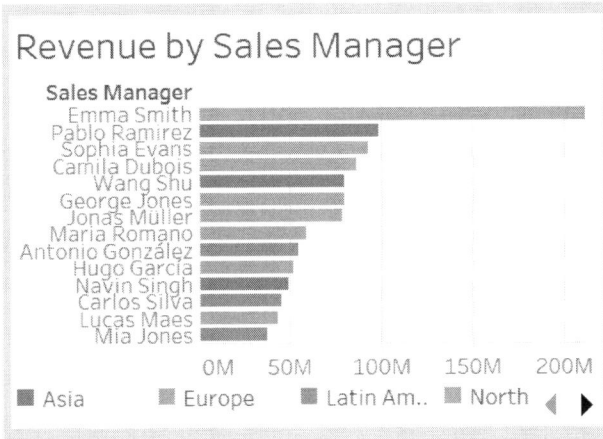

10. Right-click the chart title and click on **Format Title.**

11. Go to the sidebar, **Format Title, and Caption**, **Title**, **Shading,** and select the white color.

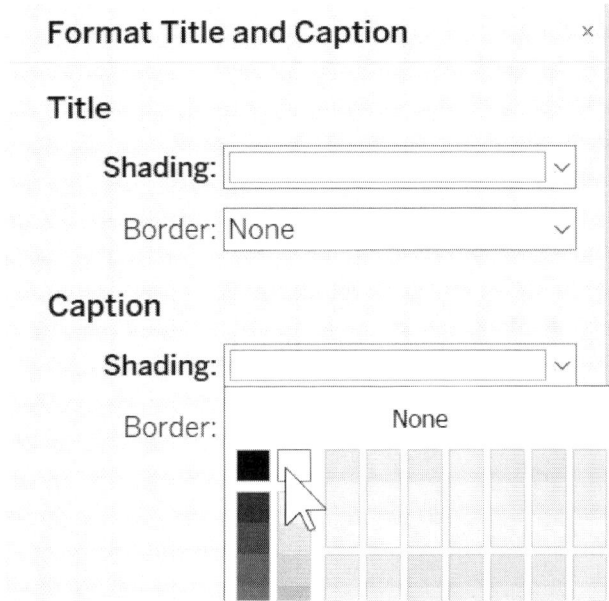

12. The Dashboard should look like the image below.

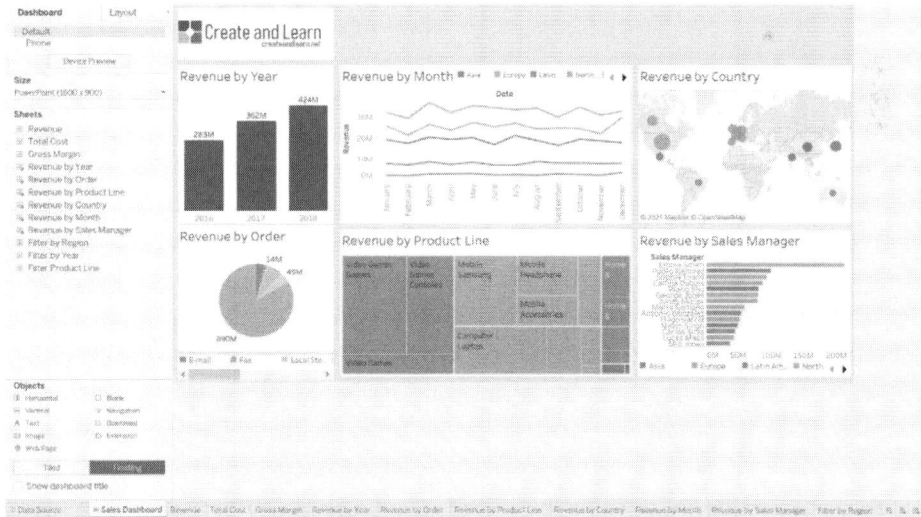

25. Add Revenue

1. Go to the **Side Bar**, **Objects,** and select **Floating**. Then, go to the **Sheets** area and double-click or drag the **Revenue** to add in the Dashboard.

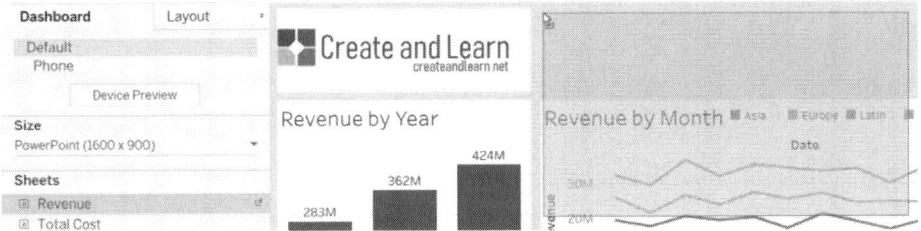

2. Go to **Layout** tab, **Position** and set the **X** to 394, **Y** to 10. Then change the size **w** to 220 and **h** to 122. Click on **Background** and change the color to white.

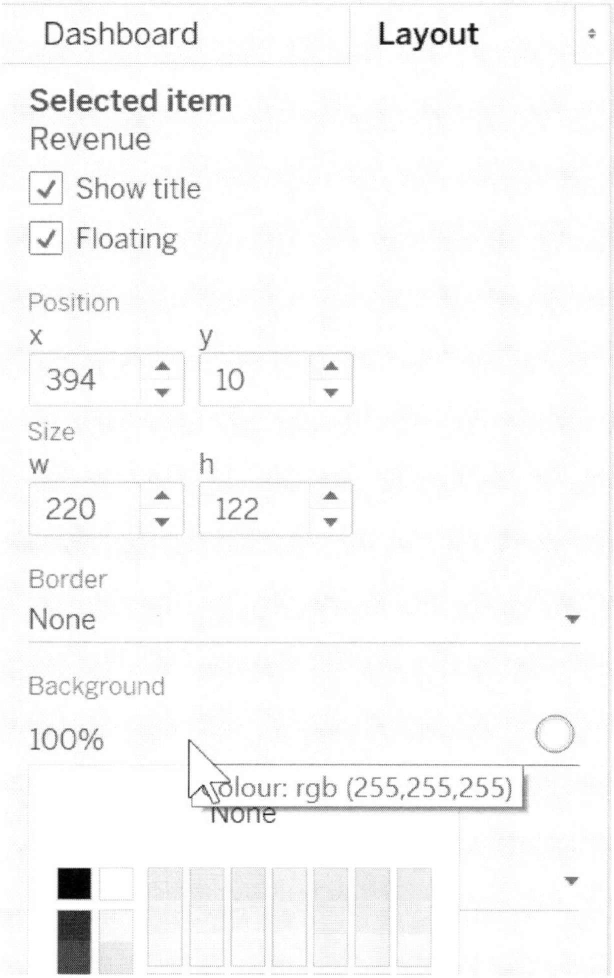

Dashboard	Layout	⇕

Selected item
Revenue

☑ Show title

☑ Floating

Position

x	y
394	10

Size

w	h
220	122

Border

None ▼

Background

100% ○

Colour: rgb (255,255,255)

None

3. Right-click the chart title and click on **Format Title**

4. Go to the sidebar, **Format Title, and Caption**, **Title**, **Shading**, and select the white color.

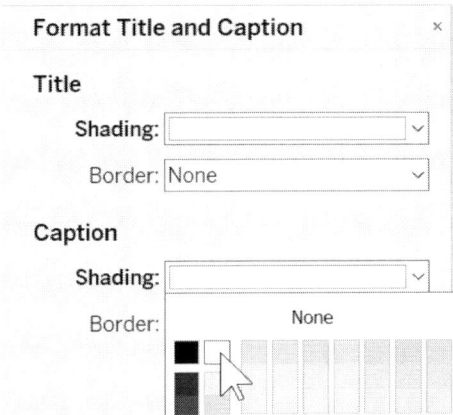

5. The Dashboard should look like the image below.

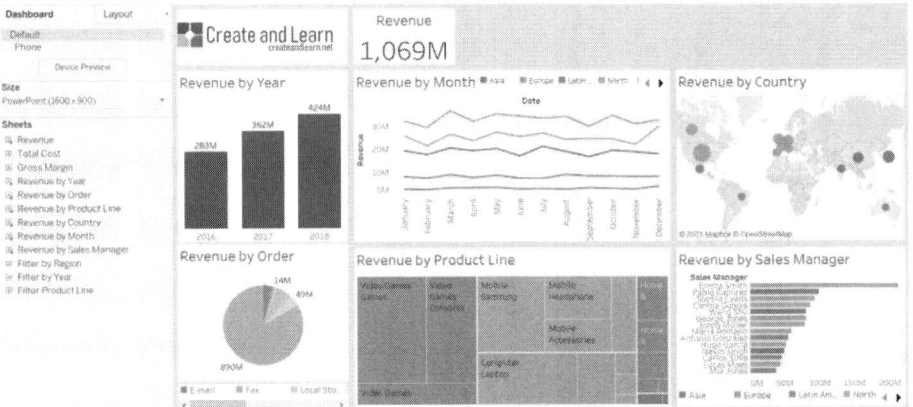

26.   Add Total Cost

1. Go to the **Side Bar**, **Objects,** and select **Floating**. Then, go to the **Sheets** area and double-click or drag the **Total Cost** to add in the Dashboard.

2. Go to **Layout** tab, **Position,** and set the **X** to 627, **Y** to 10. Then change the size **w** to 220 and **h** to 122. Click on **Background** and change the color to white.

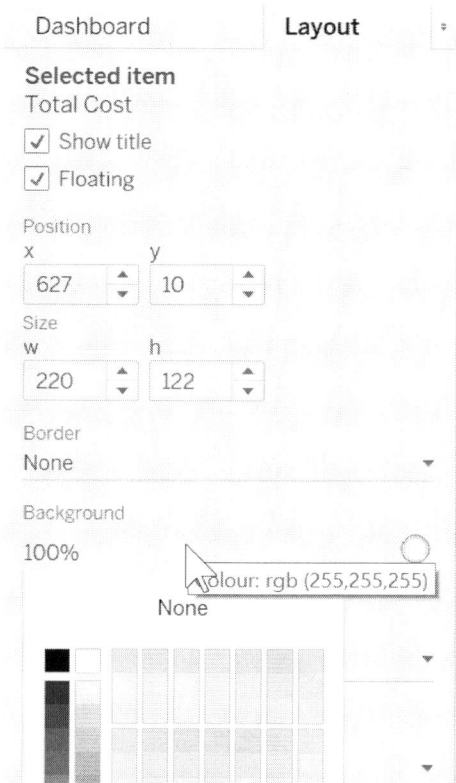

3. Right-click the chart title and click on **Format Title**

4. Go to the sidebar, **Format Title, and Caption**, **Title**, **Shading**, and select the white color.

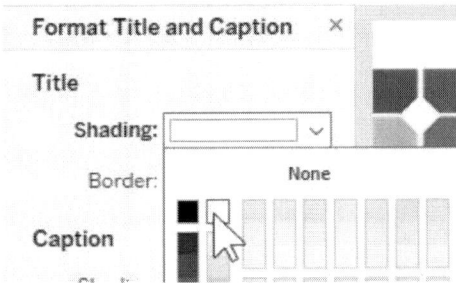

5. The Dashboard should look like the image below.

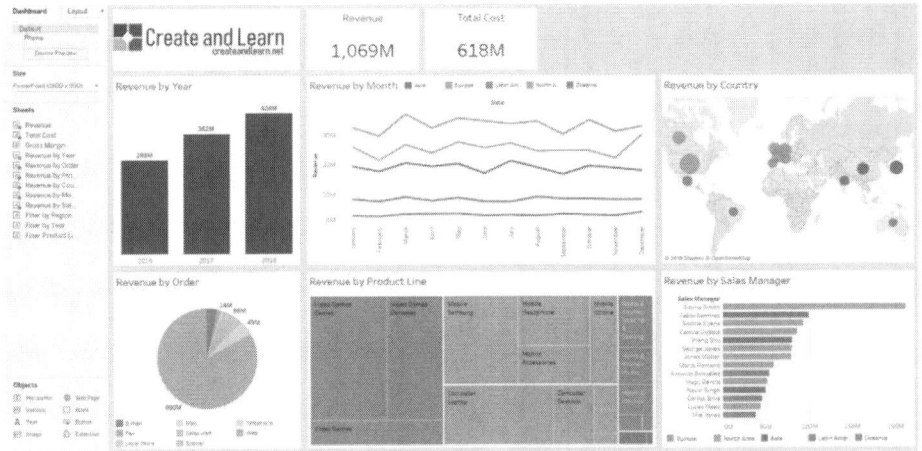

27.   Add Gross Margin

1. Go to the **Side Bar**, **Objects,** and select **Floating**. Then, go to the **Sheets** area and double-click or drag the **Gross Margin** to add to the Dashboard.

2. Go to **Layout** tab, **Position,** and set the **X** to 860, **Y** to 10. Then change the size **w** to 220 and **h** to 122. Click on **Background** and change the color to white.

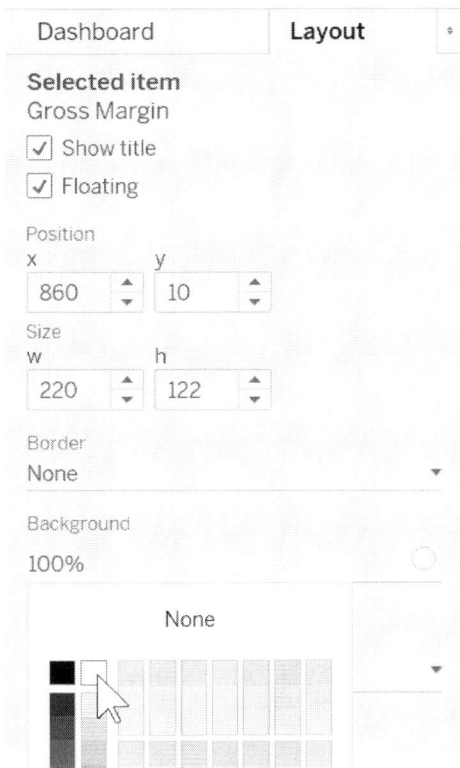

3. Right-click the chart title and click on **Format Title**

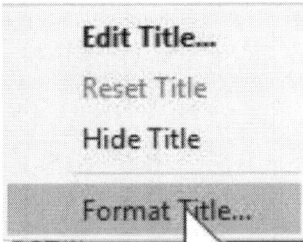

Edit Title...

Reset Title

Hide Title

Format Title...

4. Go to the sidebar, **Format Title, and Caption**, **Title**, **Shading,** and select the white color.

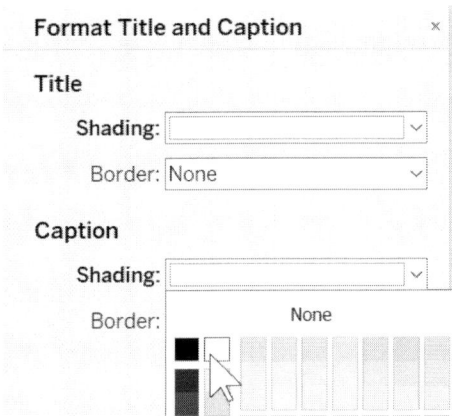

Format Title and Caption ✕

Title

Shading: [ ]

Border: None

Caption

Shading: [ ]

Border: None

5. The Dashboard should look like the image below.

28.   Add Filter – Product Line

Filter actions send information between worksheets. Typically, a filter action sends information from a selected mark to another sheet showing the piece of information you selected.

1. Go to the **Side Bar**, **Objects,** and select **Floating**. Then, go to the **Sheets** area and double-click or drag the **Filter Product Line** to add in the Dashboard.

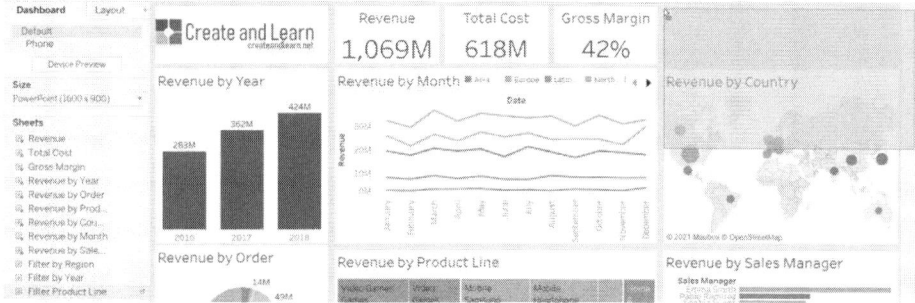

2. Go to **Layout** tab, **Position,** and set the **X** to 1096, **Y** to 10. Then change the size **w** to 219 and **h** to 122. Click on **Background** and change the color to white.

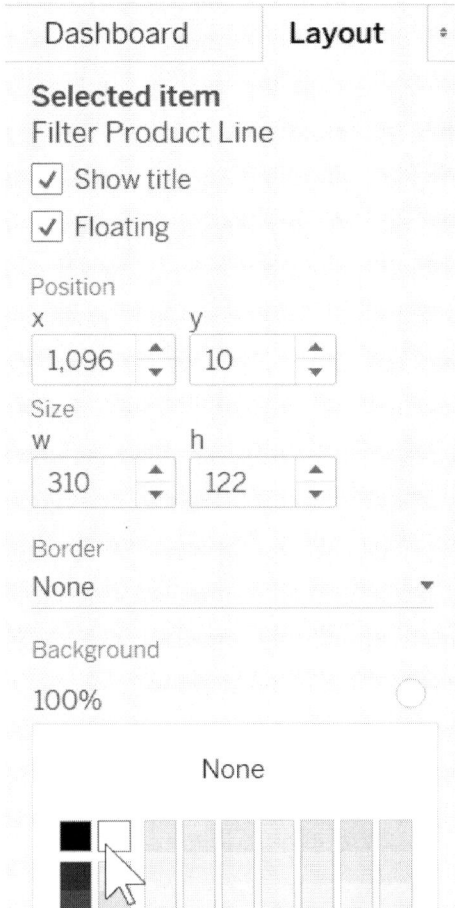

Dashboard	Layout	≑

Selected item
Filter Product Line

- ☑ Show title
- ☑ Floating

Position

x	y
1,096 ⏶⏷	10 ⏶⏷

Size

w	h
310 ⏶⏷	122 ⏶⏷

Border
None ▾

Background
100% ◯

None

3. Go to the **Toolbar**, **Fit,** and select **Entire View**.

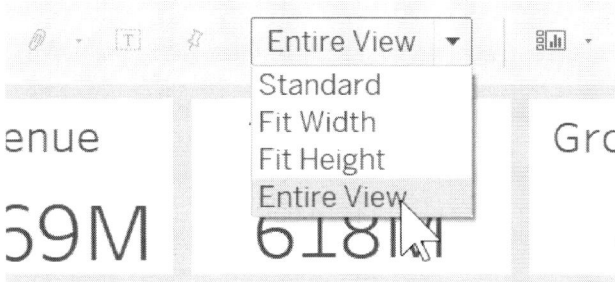

4. Click on the down-arrow and uncheck the **Title** option.

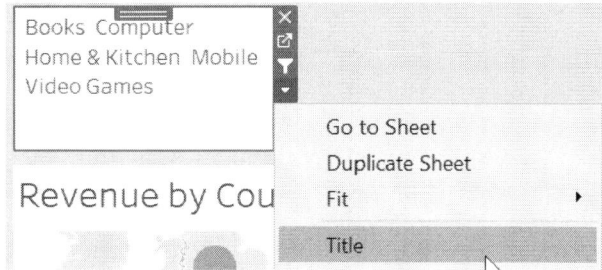

5. Check the icon **Use as Filter**.

6. Click on the texts to filter the Dashboard by Books, Computer, etc. You can hold the **ctrl key** to select multiple items. Click on the blank area of the visual to clean the filter.

If you filter by **Computer**, The Dashboard should look like the image below.

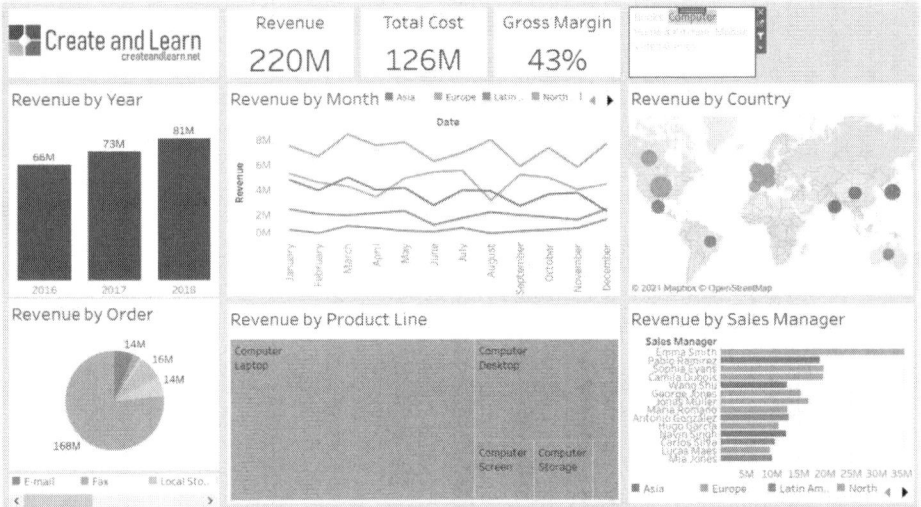

29. Add Filter – Region

1. Go to the **Side Bar**, **Objects,** and select **Floating**. Then, go to the **Sheets** area and double-click or drag the **Filter by Region** to add in the Dashboard.

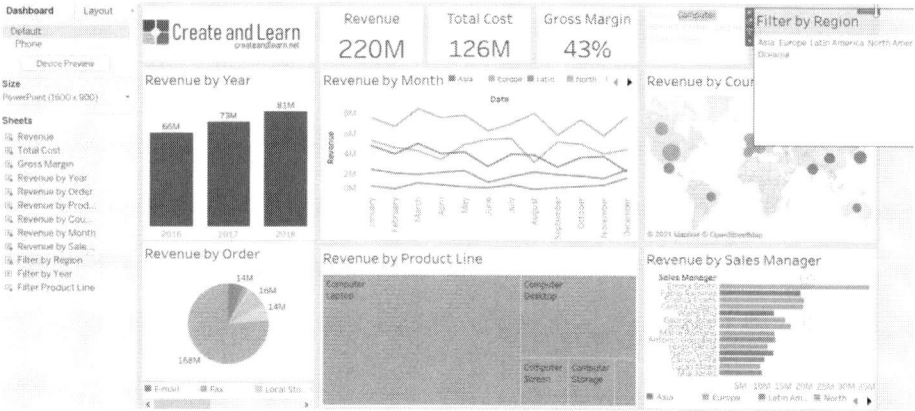

2. Go to **Layout** tab, **Position,** and set the **X** to 1330, **Y** to 10. Then change the size **w** to 263 and **h** to 87. Click on **Background** and change the color to white. Untick **Show title.**

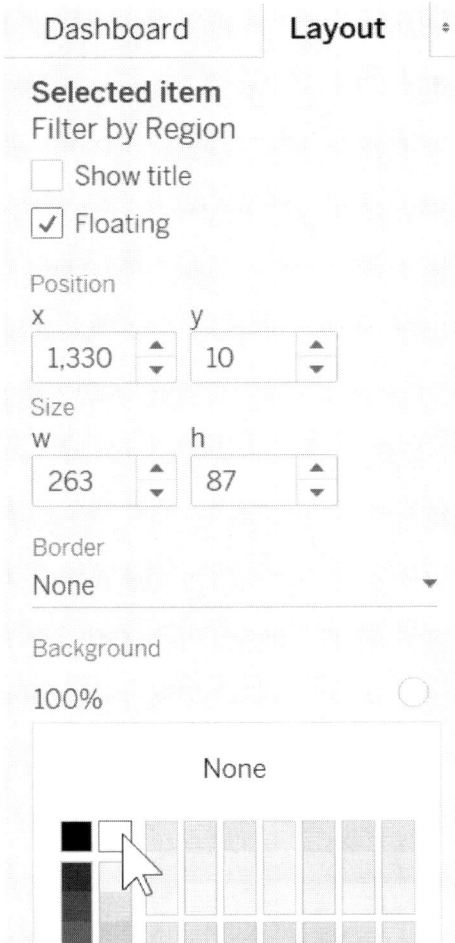

| Dashboard | **Layout** | ⇕ |

Selected item
Filter by Region

☐ Show title

☑ Floating

Position
x
1,330 ⇕   y
10 ⇕

Size
w
263 ⇕   h
87 ⇕

Border
None ▼

Background
100%   ◯

None

3. Go to the **Toolbar**, **Fit,** and select **Entire View**.

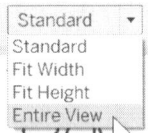

Standard ▼
Standard
Fit Width
Fit Height
Entire View

4. Check the icon **Use as Filter**.

5. If you filter by **Europe** Region, The Dashboard should look like the image below.

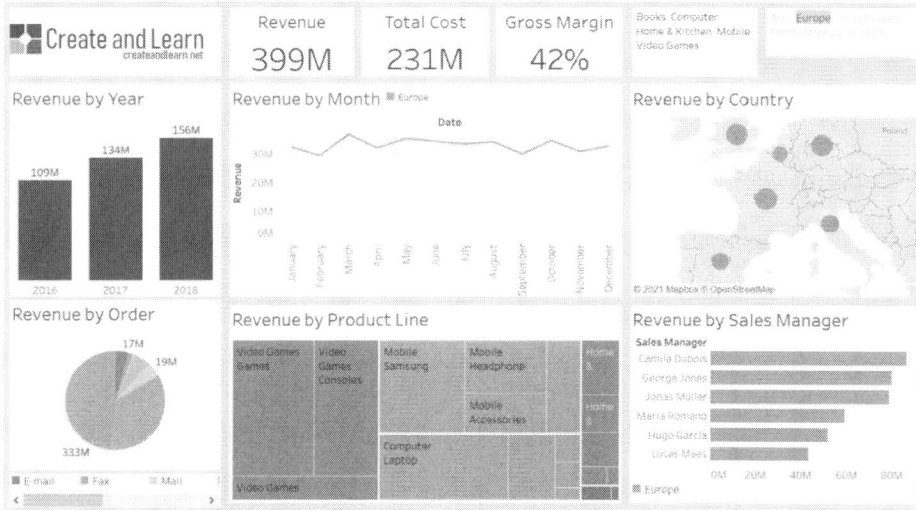

30.   Add Filter – Year

1. Go to the **Side Bar**, **Objects,** and select **Floating**. Then, go to the **Sheets** area and double-click or drag the **Filter by Year** to add in the Dashboard.

2. Go to **Layout** tab, **Position,** and set the **X** to 1330, **Y** to 98. Then change the size **w** to 263 and **h** to 34. Click on **Background** and change the color to white. Untick **Show title**.

Dashboard	Layout	÷

Selected item
Filter by Year

☐ Show title

☑ Floating

Position
x   y
| 1,330 ▲▼ | 98 ▲▼ |

Size
w   h
| 263 ▲▼ | 34 ▲▼ |

Border
None ▼

Background

100% ⬭

Colour: rgb (255,255,255)

3. Go to the **Toolbar**, **Fit,** and select **Entire View**.

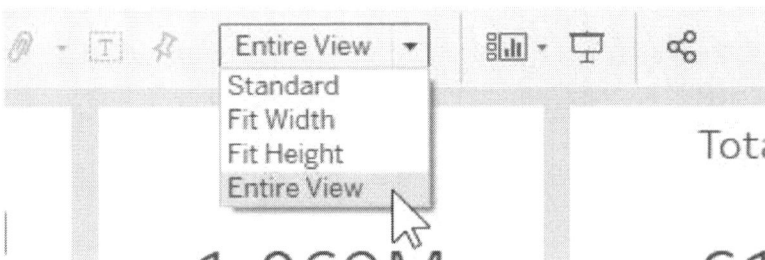

| 📎 ▾ | T | 🖈 | Entire View ▾ | 📊 ▾ | 🖥 | ⚹ |

Standard
Fit Width
Fit Height
Entire View

Tota

4. Check the icon **Use as Filter**.

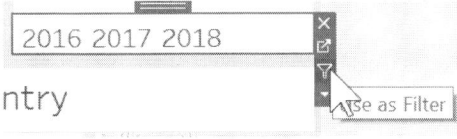

5. If you filter by **2018**, The Dashboard should look like the image below.

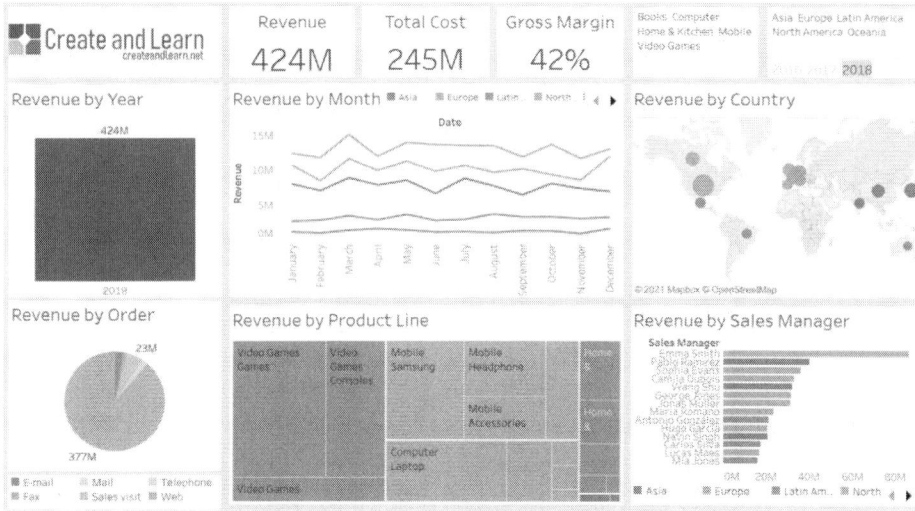

6. You will note that the chart **Revenue by Year** was filtered as well. But this one should not be filtered by year, but always show the annual comparisons.

7. To change this, go to the **Dashboard** tab and click on **Actions**.

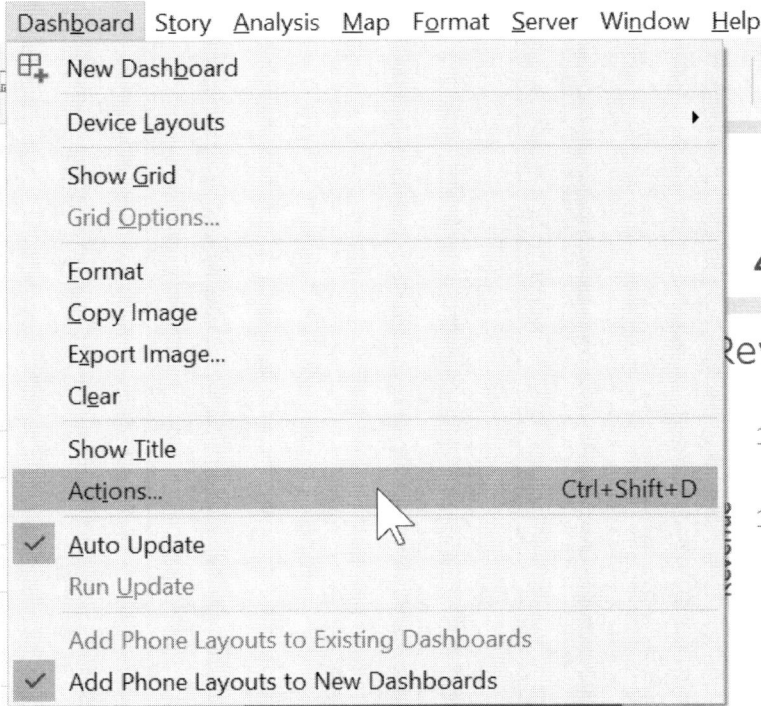

Dashboard	Story	Analysis	Map	Format	Server	Window	Help

- New Dashboard
- Device Layouts   ▶
- Show Grid
- Grid Options...

- Format
- Copy Image
- Export Image...
- Clear

- Show Title
- Actions...   Ctrl+Shift+D
- ✓ Auto Update
- Run Update

- Add Phone Layouts to Existing Dashboards
- ✓ Add Phone Layouts to New Dashboards

8. If needed, you can change the column width.

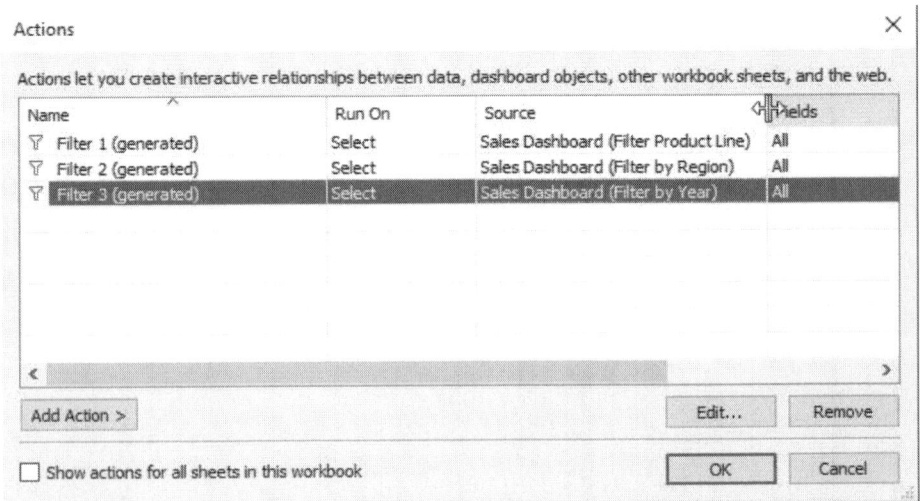

Actions   ✕

Actions let you create interactive relationships between data, dashboard objects, other workbook sheets, and the web.

Name	Run On	Source	Fields
▽ Filter 1 (generated)	Select	Sales Dashboard (Filter Product Line)	All
▽ Filter 2 (generated)	Select	Sales Dashboard (Filter by Region)	All
▽ Filter 3 (generated)	Select	Sales Dashboard (Filter by Year)	All

Add Action >   Edit...   Remove

☐ Show actions for all sheets in this workbook   OK   Cancel

9. Select the Sales Dashboard (Filtered by Year) and click on Edit.

Actions   ✕

Actions let you create interactive relationships between data, dashboard objects, other workbook sheets, and the web.

Name	Run On	Source	Fields
▽ Filter 1 (generated)	Select	Sales Dashboard (Filter Product Line)	All
▽ Filter 2 (generated)	Select	Sales Dashboard (Filter by Region)	All
▽ Filter 3 (generated)	Select	Sales Dashboard (Filter by Year)	All

Add Action >   Edit...   Remove

☐ Show actions for all sheets in this workbook   OK   Cancel

10. Go to **Target Sheets** section and uncheck the **Revenue by Year**. Then click, **OK**.

11. If you filter by the Year **2018**, The Dashboard should look like the image below.

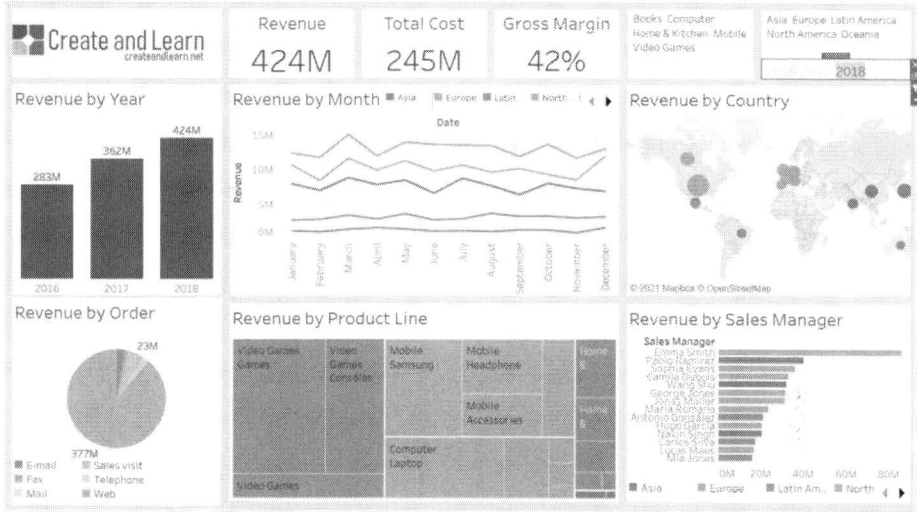

Chapter **7**

Mobile Dashboard

Phone layouts are automatically generated by default whenever you create a new dashboard. To create them only for specific dashboards, deselect Auto-Generate Phone Layouts from the Dashboard menu.

1. Go to the sidebar on the left and close any other sidebar that might be open and leave only the **Dashboard | Layout** bar.

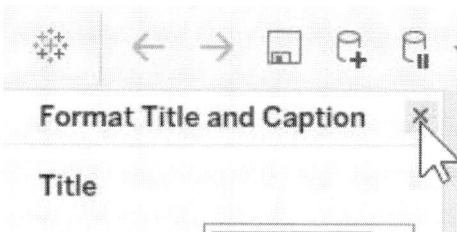

2. Go to the **Dashboard** tab and click on **Phone**. The layout will change to a phone view, and Tableau will automatically arrange the Dashboard elements.

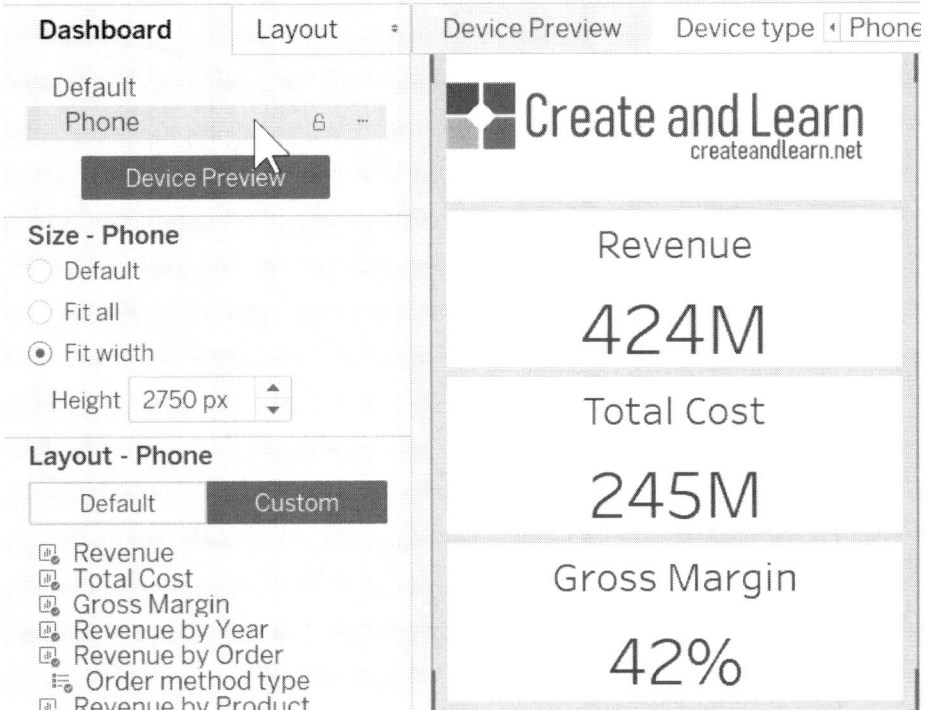

3. Go to **Phone** pop-up menu, click on the ellipsis **Edit layout.**

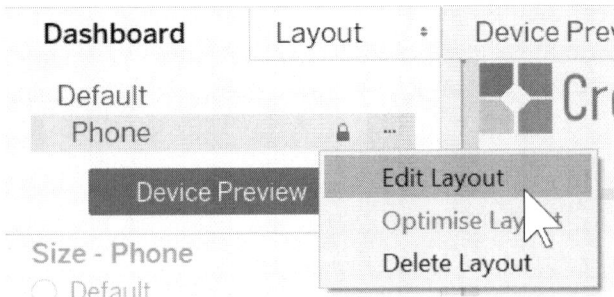

4. Click on the element and use the handle to move it across the view. Move the filters to have a result like image below.

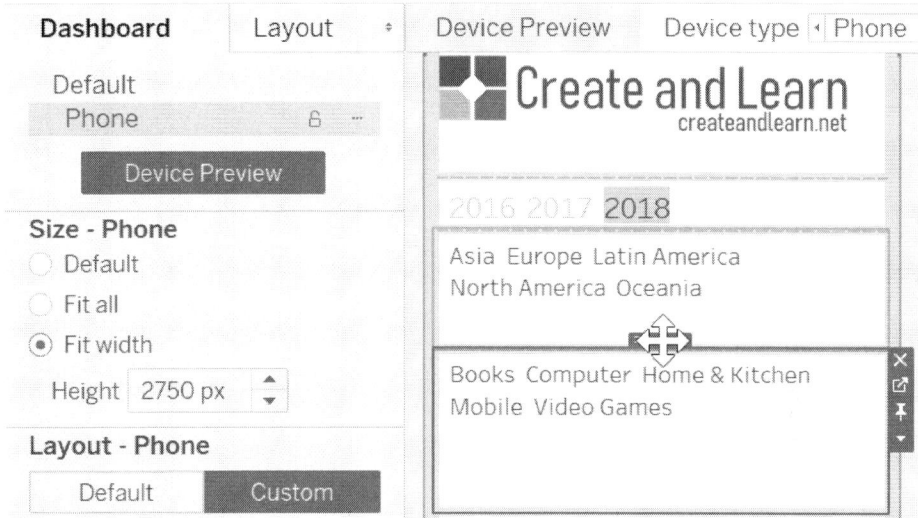

5. Go to **Dashboard** tab and click on **Device Preview**.

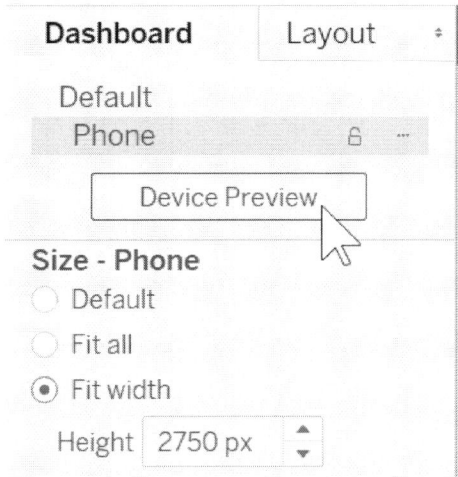

6. At the top of the Dashboard, a **Device Preview** section will be displayed with the option to change the **Device type** and **Model**. Try some options to see how your dashboard will look like on each device.

Chapter **8**

Adjustments

1. Go to the **Revenue by Order** chart and adjust the size of the **legends** to have three columns.

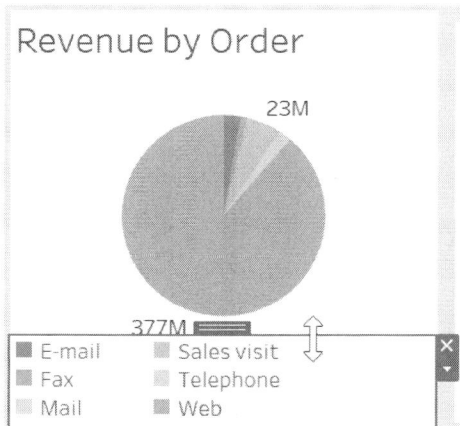

2. Click on Use as Filter.

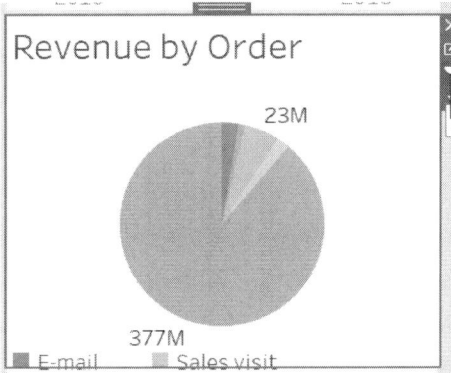

3. Go to Revenue by Product Line and click on Use as Filter.

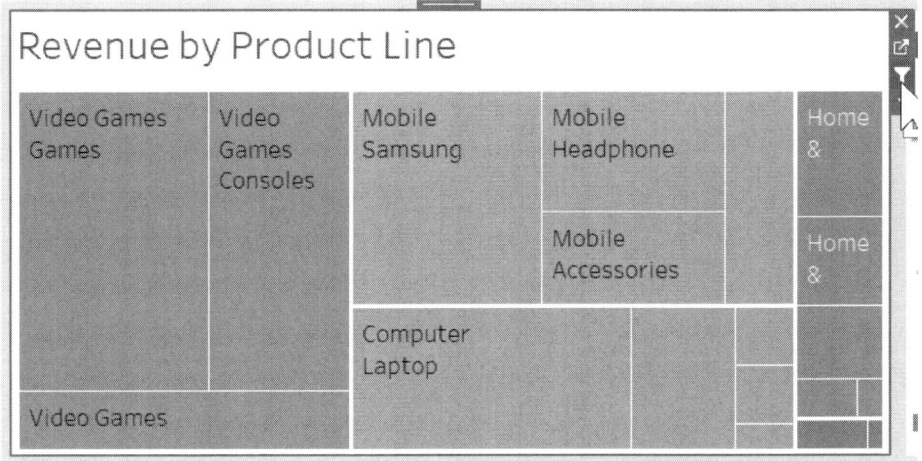

4. Go to Revenue by Sales Manager and click on Use as Filter.

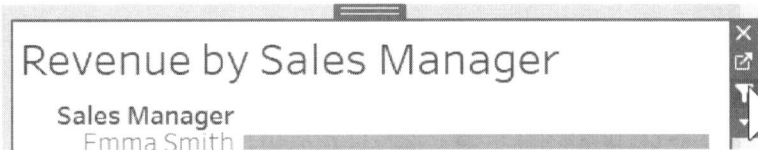

5. Go to Revenue by Country and click on Use as Filter.

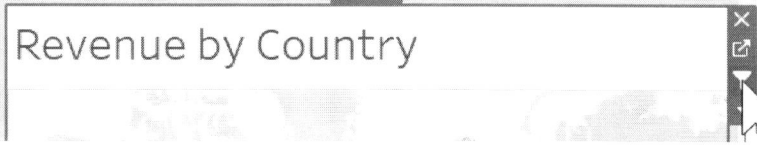

Revenue by Country

6. Go to Revenue by Month and click on Use as Filter.

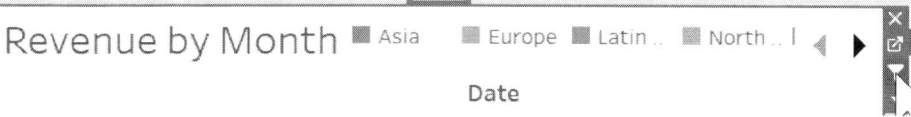

Revenue by Month ■ Asia   ■ Europe   ■ Latin ..   ■ North .. I ◄ ►

Date

7. Congratulations! Your Dashboard is finished and ready to be shared or published.

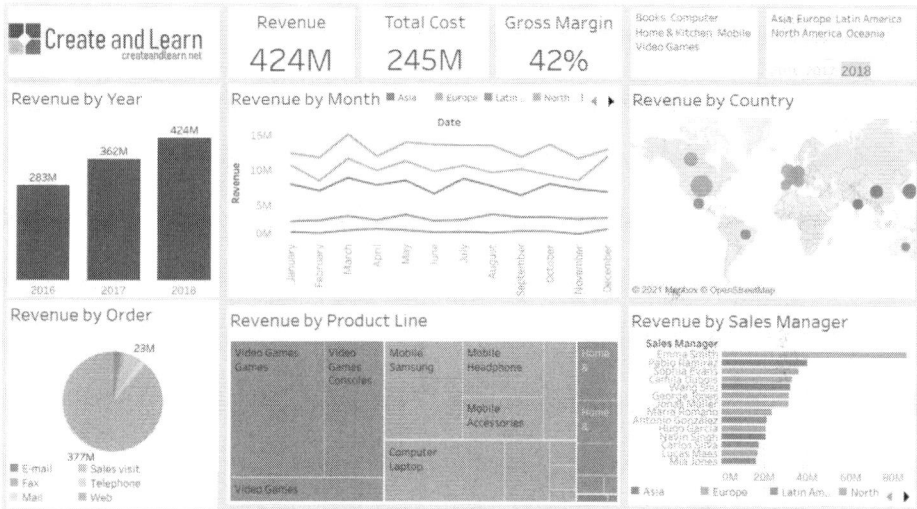

Chapter **9**

Share

In Tableau, you can share your public work on Tableau Public, social media, website, email, files; and you can share your business or confidential work with your team by publishing it to Tableau Online or Tableau Server. You and your team can then access the visuals through the Tableau mobile app or any web browser.

31. Exporting as PowerPoint

1. Go to File, click on Export AS PowerPoint.

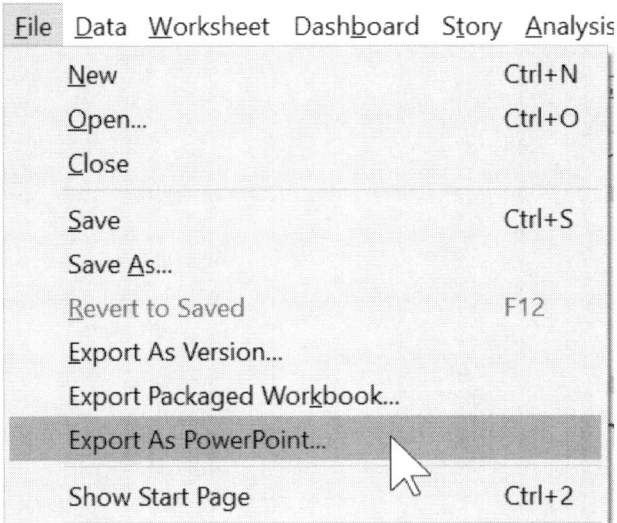

File	Data	Worksheet	Dashboard	Story	Analysis

New   Ctrl+N

Open...   Ctrl+O

Close

Save   Ctrl+S

Save As...

Revert to Saved   F12

Export As Version...

Export Packaged Workbook...

Export As PowerPoint...

Show Start Page   Ctrl+2

2. Select Specific sheets from this workbook. Then click Select All and Export.

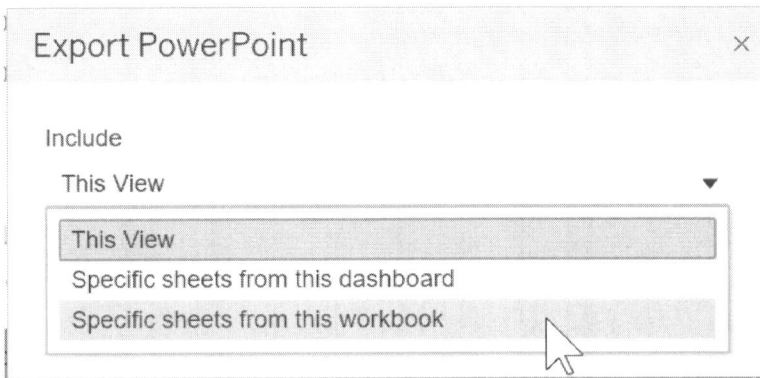

Export PowerPoint   ×

Include

This View ▼

This View
Specific sheets from this dashboard
Specific sheets from this workbook

Export PowerPoint   ✕

Include

Specific sheets from this workbook   ▼

   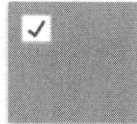

Sales Dashbo ...   Revenue   Total Cost   Gross Margin

◄   ►

13 of 13   **Select All**   **Clear All**

Export

3. Give the name **biClinic.pptx** . Then, click on **Save**.

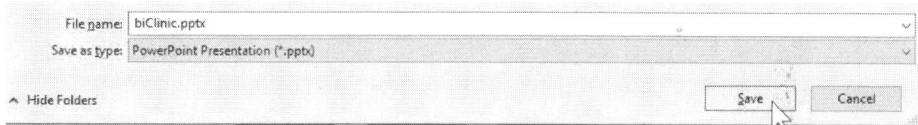

4. Open the biClinic.pptx file.

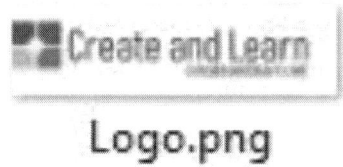

biClinic.pptx

Logo.png

5. Tableau will save each tab from your workbook as a single slide making it easy to share or reuse in your presentations.

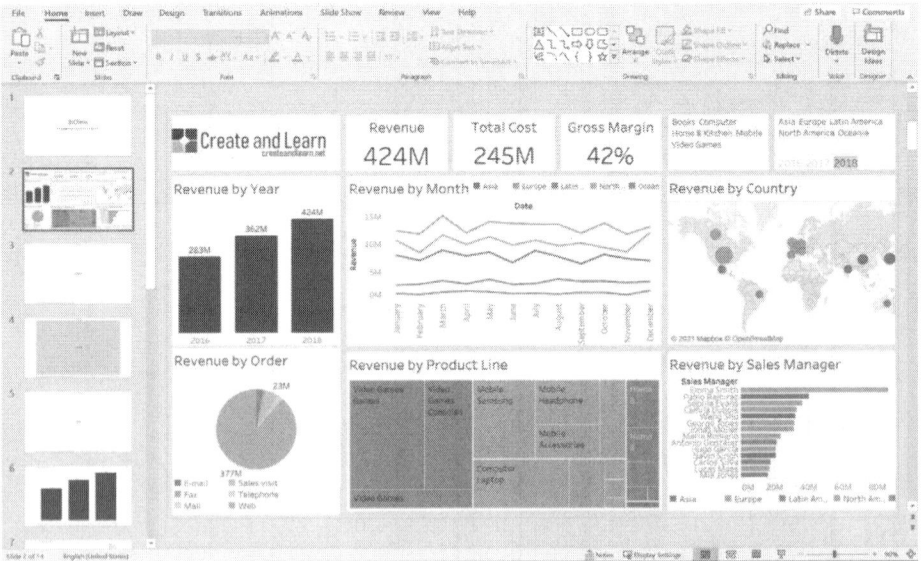

32.   Exporting as PDF

1. Go to **File** and click on **Print to PDF**.

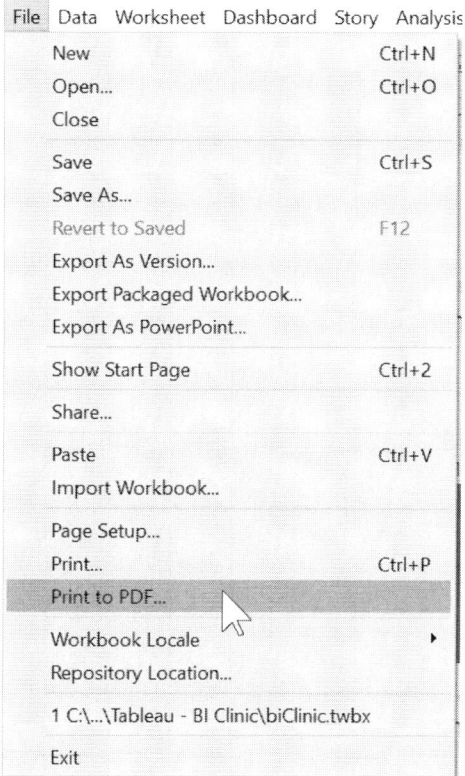

File	Data	Worksheet	Dashboard	Story	Analysis

New   Ctrl+N
Open...   Ctrl+O
Close

Save   Ctrl+S
Save As...
Revert to Saved   F12
Export As Version...
Export Packaged Workbook...
Export As PowerPoint...

Show Start Page   Ctrl+2

Share...

Paste   Ctrl+V
Import Workbook...

Page Setup...
Print...   Ctrl+P
Print to PDF...

Workbook Locale   ▶
Repository Location...

1 C:\...\Tableau - BI Clinic\biClinic.twbx

Exit

2. Now, let's export the Dashboard tab only. When the **Print to PDF** window opens, select **Active sheet**, **Landscape,** and click **OK**.

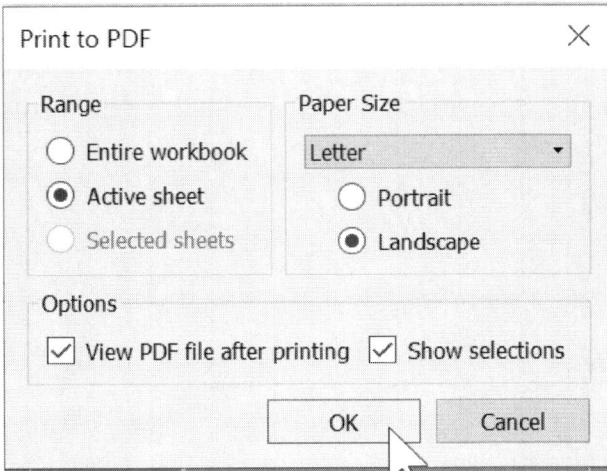

Print to PDF   ✕

Range
- ○ Entire workbook
- ● Active sheet
- ○ Selected sheets

Paper Size
Letter ▾
- ○ Portrait
- ● Landscape

Options
- ☑ View PDF file after printing   ☑ Show selections

OK   Cancel

3. Give the name **biClinic.pdf** . Then, click on **Save**.

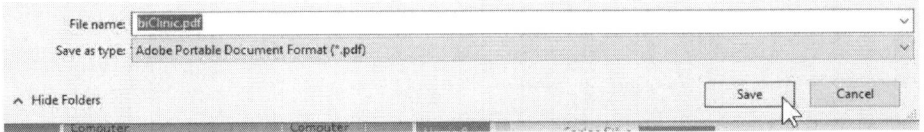

File name: biClinic.pdf

Save as type: Adobe Portable Document Format (*.pdf)

∧ Hide Folders   Save   Cancel

4. The PDF file should have one page with the Dashboard.

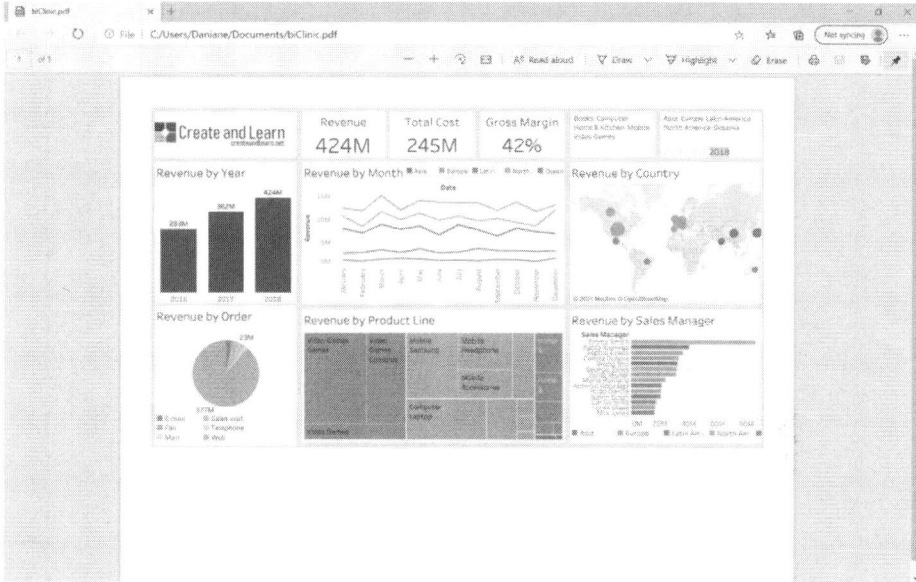

33. Export as Version

1. Go to **File** and click on **Export As Version**.

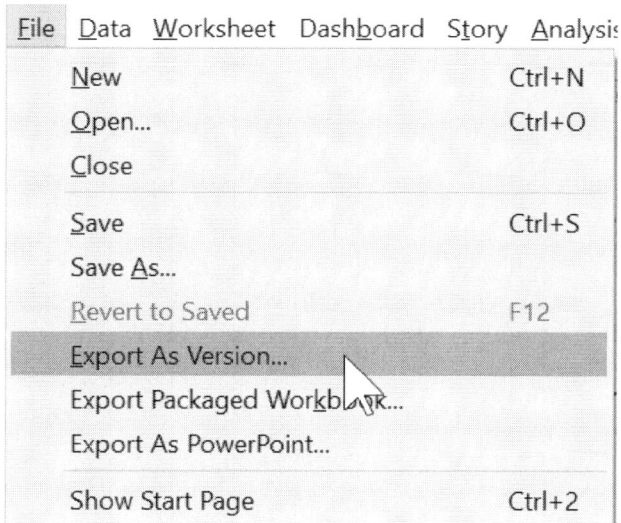

2. You can select previous Tableau versions to export your workbook.

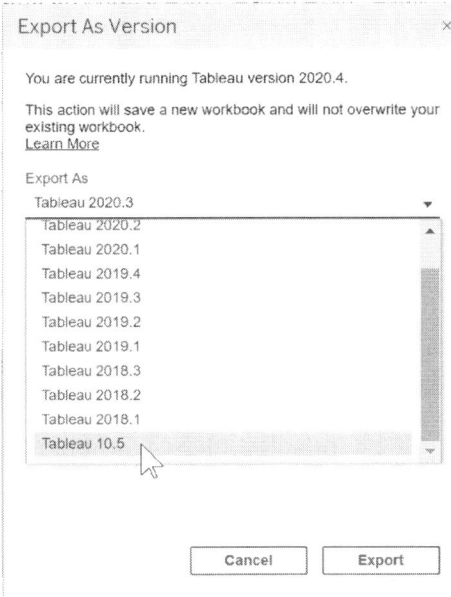

Export As Version   ×

You are currently running Tableau version 2020.4.

This action will save a new workbook and will not overwrite your existing workbook.
Learn More

Export As

Tableau 2020.3   ▼

Tableau 2020.2
Tableau 2020.1
Tableau 2019.4
Tableau 2019.3
Tableau 2019.2
Tableau 2019.1
Tableau 2018.3
Tableau 2018.2
Tableau 2018.1
Tableau 10.5

Cancel   Export

34.   Publishing to Tableau Public

Tableau Public is exactly what it says **PUBLIC**. This is a free service that lets you publish your visuals to the web. You can then embed the visuals into webpages, share via social media or email, etc.

Confidential and Business data should be shared in the private and controlled versions of Tableau like Tableau Online or Tableau Server.

1. Go to **Server, Tableau Public** and click on **Save to Tableau Public As**.

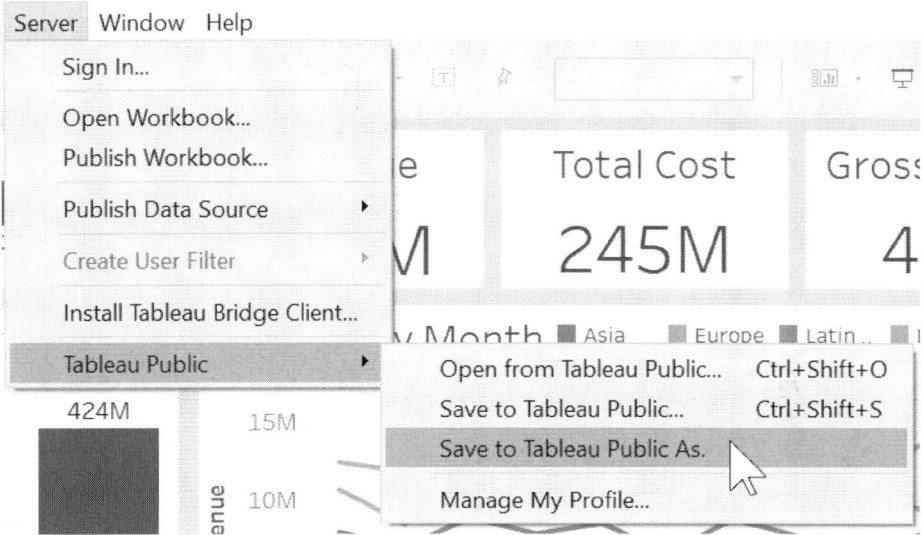

3. The Tableau Sign In window will appear. You can create a free account by clicking on **Create one now for free**. Or you can use your credentials if you have one. Go ahead and sign with your new or current account.

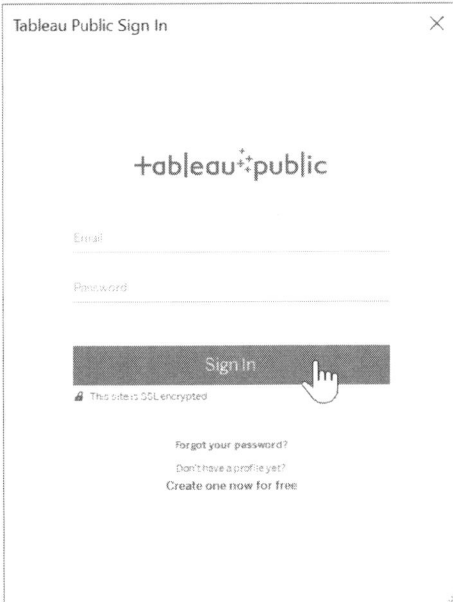

4. After you **Sign In** tableau will start saving the workbook in Tableau Public.

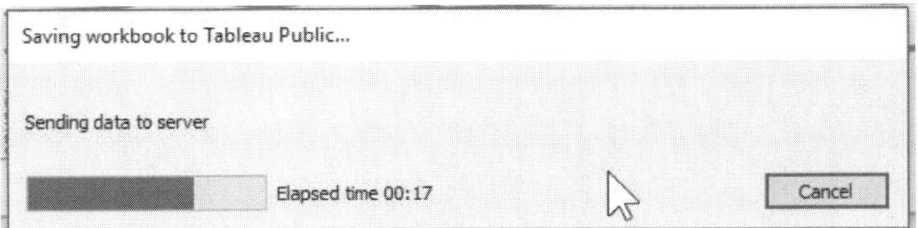

5. Once completed, your Dashboard will be available in Tableau Public, and everyone will be able to access and see your work.

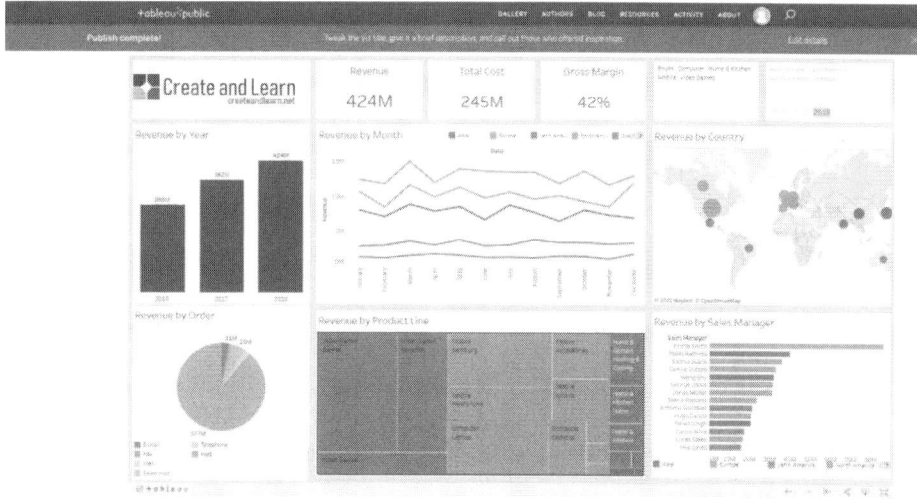

6. To share the Dashboard, click on **Share**.

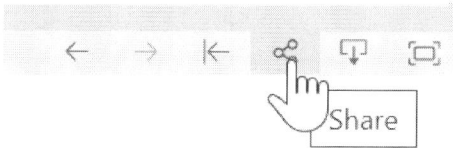

7. In the **Share** window, you have multiple options to share the Dashboard. You can use the **Embed Code**, **Link**, **Email**, **Twitter**, and **Facebook**.

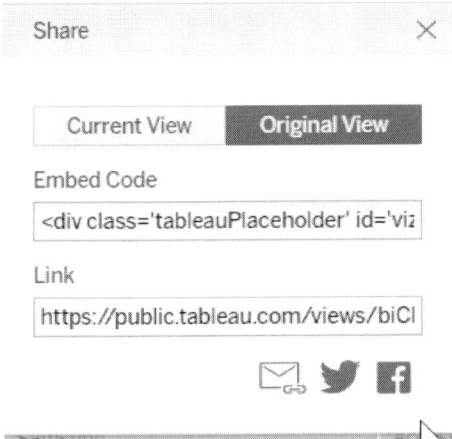

8. The example below is the Dashboard shared on my website using the **Embed Code**. Visit the website to check how it looks like https://www.createandlearn.net/tableau

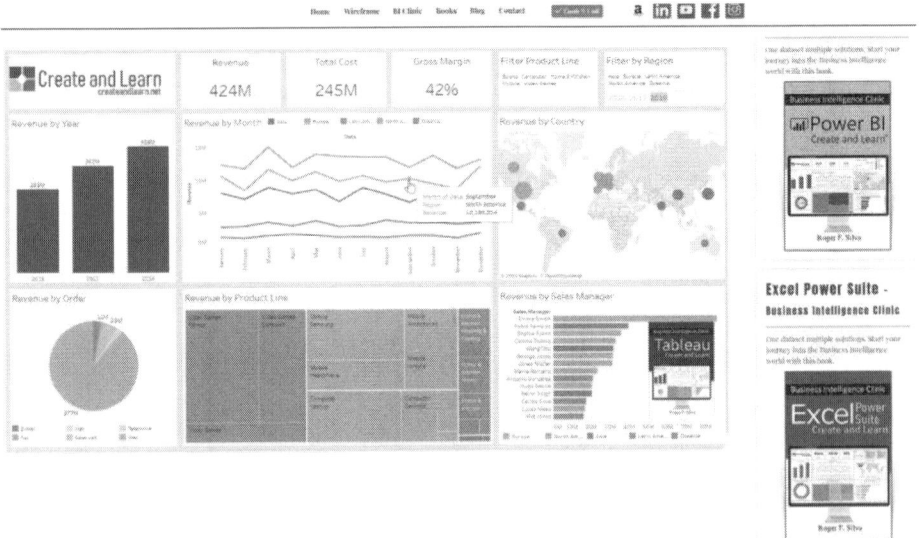

9. After you upload your Dashboard in Tableau, share it through your social media with the hashtag **#createandlearn**, I am following this

hashtag on Facebook, LinkedIn, and Instagram; I am looking forward to seeing your work and comment.

10. Also, consider **following me**, and let me know about your published work so I can follow you as well. My Tableau Public page is https://public.tableau.com/profile/createandlearn

11. Congratulations, you have created and published a professional and eye-catching sales dashboard using Tableau!

Final words

Thank you for the journey! I hope that you have enjoyed and learned from this book.

Although the Business Intelligence concept is not new, the tools and methods have changed dramatically in recent years, and you took the right decision to get more knowledge about this.

Also, I would like to ask you to take a minute to **review my book**. A good rating and your positive feedback are incredibly important for my work. If you have any comments or suggestions, please send me an email or a message on LinkedIn — I will be more than happy to hear from you and have you on my network.

Again, take a minute to review my book on the store website from which you bought it, and send me a message with your feedback if you want.

⭐⭐⭐⭐⭐

Thank you for the time we spent creating and learning.

Roger F. Silva

contact.createandlearn@gmail.com
createandlearn.net
www.linkedin.com/in/roger-f-silva

You can find more Create and Learn books, files, articles, and videos:

https://www.createandlearn.net/

https://www.amazon.com/Roger-F-Silva/e/B07JC8J1L5/

http://www.facebook.com/createandlearn.net

https://www.linkedin.com/company/create-and-learn

https://www.instagram.com/createandlearn_net/

https://www.youtube.com/c/createandlearn

For more **Create and Learn** books and articles visit:
www.createandlearn.net

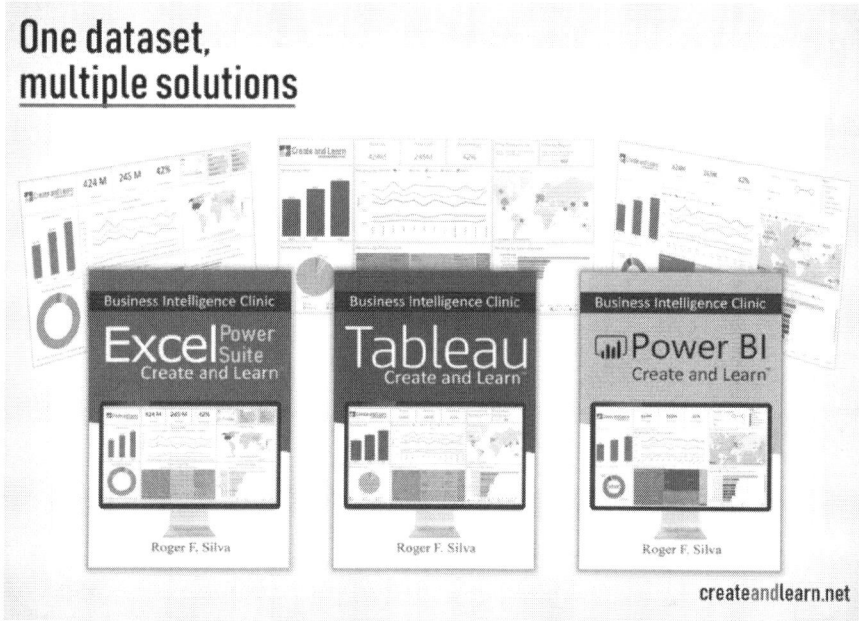

Printed in Great Britain
by Amazon

87460584R00112